OPEN ROAD'S BEST OF

Guatemala

by Bruce Morris

Open Road Travel Guides
For the amount of time you really have for your trip!

Open Road Publishing

Open Road's new travel guides cut to the chase. You don't need a huge travel encyclopedia – you need a *selective guide* to steer you right. If you're going on vacation for a few weeks or less, get a guide that brings you the *best* of any destination for the amount of time you *really* have for your trip!

Open Road – the guide you need for the trip you want.

The New Open Road *Best Of* Travel Guides.
Right to the point.
Uncluttered.
Easy.

Open Road Publishing
P.O. Box 284, Cold Spring Harbor, NY 11724
www.openroadguides.com

Text Copyright©2010 by Bruce Morris
Maps by Bruce Morris
- All Rights Reserved -

ISBN 13: 9781593601263
ISBN 10: 1-59360-126-3
Library of Congress Control No. 2009924893

About the Author
Bruce Morris is also the author of Open Road's Best of Panama, Open Road's Best of the Florida Keys & Everglades, and co-authof of Open Road's Best of Costa Rica.

For photo credits turn to page 207.

CONTENTS

MAPS

1. INTRODUCTION

This is the part of the book where I need to convince you, the reader, about the charms of **Guatemala**. It's easy to sell Guatemala. I've made a handy list of things about the country that make it so attractive to visitors. Just read it and you'll run right out and buy a plane ticket immediately.

Guatemala packs a lot of punch in a small country. It's about the size of Cuba, Tennessee or roughly three times the size of Wales. There are **numerous attractions in a small area**, and good transportation infrastructure.

Guatemala is one of the most colorful countries in the world. Not only does it enjoy a lush tropical landscape littered with exotic flowers, but the majority of the people dress in brightly-colored traditional *huipiles* and pantaloons.

Guatemala enjoys a well-developed **infrastructure**. It's a modern country with good roads, telecommunications and good banking and business services. There are major airports in Guatemala City and near Tikal at Flores.

Flights from the US are cheap. It's **only a four-hour flight** from Houston—closer than many Caribbean destinations.

Guatemala is not a sleeper tourism destination. As travel to Central America grows, travel to Guatemala is booming. Retirees from all over the world discovered it many years ago. Gringos from Europe, North America and South Africa and Latinos from all

over South America are making Guatemala their new home. Hippies left over from the sixties linger in Xela and around Lake Atitlán.

I hate to use trite clichés, but here goes: **Guatemala is the new Costa Rica**. I love both countries. But the things that attract the growing tourist hordes to Costa Rica are all present in Guatemala, in profusion and with far less tourist traffic – and cheaper, too.

2. OVERVIEW

Guatemala City

Guatemala City has earned a reputation as being unsafe, dirty and uninteresting. Not so. The city is made up of three main areas. The Central Historic District, *Centro Histórico*, which is mostly Zone 1, the newer part of town known as the *Zona Viva* or Zone 10, and all the rest. The population is officially 4 million but is likely much more. The vast majority of the people live outside the center. As a visitor you should undoubtedly **concentrate your time in Zones 1 and 10**.

Antigua

Extremely quaint, almost, as the British would say, twee, **Antigua** is swarming with colorful *indígenas* and students from all over the world. A **World Heritage site**, Antigua is colorful with colonial architecture rivaling the old city in Havana, Cuba or Cartagena, Columbia. Dozens of centuries-old churches litter the town. Some are little more than shells having lost their roof to the numerous earthquakes that have shaped the city and its history. There is a lively music scene, art galleries, trendy res-

taurants, groovy bars, happening dance clubs, bohemian poetry readings and more! Hundreds of students on multiple-week Spanish immersion courses pack the town bringing a youthful, international vibe.

Lake Atitlán

One of the most beautiful sights in the world, rivaling Italy's Lake Como or the Grand Canyon,

volcano-surrounded **Lake Atitlán** is chock-a-block with bohemian types, artists, musicians, new age vortex watchers and regular old gringo tourists. Great restaurants, lively bars and a couple of the nicest hotels in the country make Lake Atitlán one of the most memorable stops on visitors' Guatemalan itinerary. Colorful indigenous Mayans weave and wear brilliantly-colored fabrics. Yes, you get a chance to buy some.

Chichicastenango

A riot of color awaits visitors to the **largest and most famous market in Central America**. Market days are Thursday and Sunday. Sunday markets are usually larger and, on Sundays of particular significance, loud, crazily-costumed, almost wild religious processions thread their way through the crowds. It's very cool. This has been a highland market village for centuries. Get your cameras and money ready.

Chichicastenango is also the gateway to the **Verapaces Highlands** and the little-touristed Cobán-coffee mecca.

Tikal

The largest excavated Maya ruin anywhere, **Tikal's mysterious beauty** enchants travelers. Surrounded by and engulfed in thick tropical jungle, the enormous snouts of the **Mayan temples** rise above the trees. As you gaze

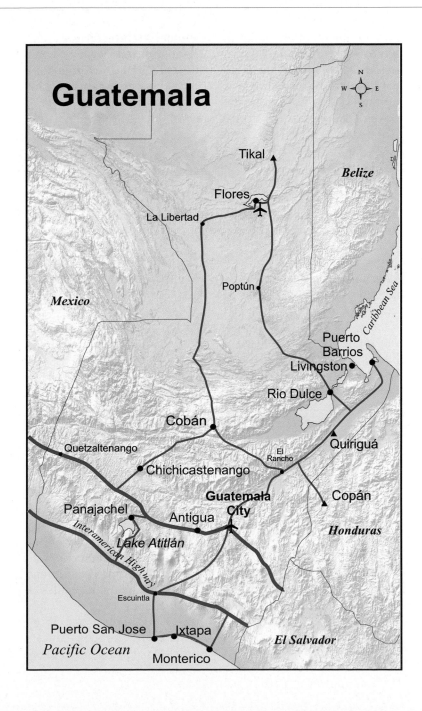

out over the miles and miles of rainforest surrounding the extensive ruins, it is difficult to imagine that the wilderness is fairly new. This used to be the Mayan Los Angeles. Easy to get to and easy to enjoy, Tikal is one of the major tourist destinations in Central America.

Copán

The Mayan ruins of **Copán** in neighboring Honduras are one of the most interesting pre-Columbian sites in Central America. The city was a Mayan cultural capital, and it's richer in sculptures, hieroglyphics and art treasures than any other known Mayan site. The famous Plaza of the Jaguars hints at exotic rituals designed to take worshippers on a journey into the underworld. The ruins are an easy side trip from Guatemala City or Antigua. Although it would be a little rushed, day trips can be arranged.

Mayan Ruins

Numerous, accessible Mayan sites are scattered all over the country. The magnificent **Quiriguá** sports superb stelae. Chuitinamit, Iximché, Mixco, Monte Alto, Cancuén and others are easy to get to. For the more adventurous, enormous, mostly unexplored Mayan cities lurk far in the jungle.

Colonial Architecture

The Spanish left a legacy of beautiful architecture. In **Antigua** and other cities, you can see some grand and imposing cathedrals and churches. In the highlands,

you can wander through delightful villages of tile roofs and cobblestone streets, with spectacular views and a perfect tropical mountain climate.

Pacific Coast

Guatemala's Pacific coast has been discovered by the big boys of sport fishing. It is probably the number one destination for sailfish. Marlin, tuna, wahoo and other sport fish attract international anglers to several, top-quality fishing lodges. Wild, brown sand beaches attract hordes of weekenders to **Ixtapa**,

Monterico and to the run-down **Puerto San Jose**. Surfers head to **Sipacate** for good quality breaks. Miles of deserted beaches line the coast but few roads lead to these paradises.

Caribbean Coast

Livingston is one of the last, almost "undiscovered" hip, cool, spots in the Caribbean. The weather is balmy, the sea is warm, the culture and food are intense reflecting a mixture of African, Mayan, and colonial Spanish and Hindu ethnicity combined with the latest reggae and *regatón* sounds. The island life is slow: dogs sleep soundly in the middle of the *Calle Principal*, main street. Local Rastafarians puff ganja and bop to sounds only they can hear.

Nightlife & Entertainment

Fine restaurants, casinos, nightclubs and bordellos of all hues and a few old favorites like Hooters and Hard Rock keep Guatemala City hopping well past dawn. There are numerous live music venues in the historic center in Guatemala City and dozens more in the Zona Viva.

Location:	Central America
Land Area:	65,000 square miles, about the size of Tennessee
Highest Point:	13,845 feet (Volcán Tajamulco)
Population:	15 million
Climate:	Tropical
Biodiversity:	8,681 plant species, +/-700 bird species, 5 endangered species
Languages:	Spanish, English, 21 Mayan, Garífuna, Xinca, and Caribbean patois
Literacy:	71%
Life Expectancy:	70 years
Poverty Rate:	29%
Government:	Constitutional Democratic Republic
Independence:	1821
Economy:	GDP: $70 billion, 12% inflation

GUATEMALA FACTS

Antigua, Atitlán and Livingston all offer multiple venues for live music. Many nightclubs and discos double as hangouts for professional (or sometimes amateur) ladies looking for (paid) companionship.

There are several Guatemalan bands performing rock, reggae, and various forms of Latin music. Perhaps the best known band in the country is the wonderful **Bohemia Suburbana** featuring the manic singer and guitar player **Giovanni Pinzón**. The group often opens for touring international acts and habitually fills concert venues on their own. They play a laid back style of Latin rock popular with the university crowd. If they are playing anywhere near where you are staying, don't miss them. They are quite good.

Surfing

Although not yet considered a hot surf destination, the Pacific coast has a couple of excellent breaks, particularly **Sipacate**. Most of the coastline is inaccessible due to lack of roads paralleling the coast. Many excellent surf spots remain more-or-less undiscovered, or at least unadvertised. Adventurous surfers hike miles to rarely surfed breaks and bunk with locals in their homes sleeping in hammocks.

Fishing

Avid anglers aching for **sailfish** swarm to Guatemala's **Pacific coast**. A half-dozen upscale fishing lodges (usually booked solid) take punters offshore where vast schools of sails, tuna, dorado, marlin and other pelagics swarm. You are almost guaranteed to

hook up with twenty or more sails a day. The wonderful fishing conditions and huge numbers of hungry sailfish on Guatemala's Pacific coast are common themes on Saturday morning TV fishing shows and glossy monthly newsstand fishing magazines drawing hardcore anglers from all over the word. The lodges and boats are nice. The weather is great. There is probably no other place in the world where catch and release sailfish average 20 per boat, per day. Just about year round. Good deal.

Spanish Language Immersion Schools

There are hundreds of Spanish language schools in Guatemala. While most of them are located in **Antigua**, there are plenty to choose from in Guatemala City, Atitlán, Xela and almost any other popular location you can think of. Some schools are big with dozens of students and some are small with only one or two. Go to www.guatemala365.com; they do an excellent job of describing and rating the various schools.

Home stays with local families are usually considered to be a part of the "immersion learning" experience but many students stay in hotels or rent apartments. Host families generally offer private rooms, hot showers and two or three meals with the family every day. Obviously, some home stays are better than others. Most schools monitor the host families to be sure students are well housed and comfortable. Some of the host families may actually have an interest in socializing with their guests. Keep in mind though, that the families are in it for the extra income.

Almost all the schools feature **one-on-one teaching**. Most of the schools give four hours of instruction in either the morning or afternoon and students spend the rest of their day in organized activities, additional instruction or just having fun. Some schools offer curriculum specializing in medical, law, business or engineering.

This is a good way to improve your Spanish by a leap or a bound.

Bird Watching

With **over 700 species** identified, Guatemala is one of the top bird watching destinations on the planet. This is one of the best

places to track down a resplendent quetzal. While not as thick with experienced bird guides as Panama or Costa Rica, several authoritative guides can be hired, especially in the Petén area. Waterfowl are particularly well-represented along the Pacific coast.

Colorful Clothing!

There are lots of indigenous people running around wearing brightly-colored, almost to the point of gaudy, fabrics wrapped all over them. They seem to be wearing a dozen or so different pieces of cloth. Many of the women seem to be so obsessed with the need to drape themselves with multiple pieces of stunning fabrics that they wear piles of more cloth folded up on top of their heads as well. Now, this is mostly women. There are plenty of men wearing traditional garb, but the women—from very young girls to doddering grannies—are the stars of the show. In my opinion they are the stars of the country.

Climate

The higher elevations, where many of the most interesting places to visit are, are pleasantly cool all year long. One of the biggest surprises for most first time visitors is how nice and cool it is all the time; it's not hot like the tropics is supposed to be. This means you can do all sorts of outdoor things without wilting. The Caribbean and Pacific coasts boast the wonderful and interesting weather of all tropical paradises. Trade winds tend to keep things cool and there are no hurricanes or other annoying weather.

Of course it rains during the **rainy season** (June-September) in typical tropical downpours, but what are you gonna do? Even the most open-air beachfront, no doors, no windows, bar will have the standard tropical thatched roof. So you stay dry.

Safety

Antigua and the other parts of Guatemala are as safe as most of North America or Europe. Although there is poverty, there is a large and growing prosperous middle class. **Street crime is rare.**

Guatemalans are friendly and outgoing. They are tourist- and gringo-friendly. The average Guatemalan has a good impression of Americans and is curious about visitors. *Para servirle,* to serve you, is always on their tongue and defines the friendly, almost humble attitude most *Guatemaltecos* display in their daily lives.

Ecotourism

Ecotourism is just beginning in Guatemala. Approximately 25% of Guatemala is still forested – secondary forest. There is very little primary forest left anywhere in the country. **About 27% of Guatemala's area is preserved in government or privately operated preserves.** Birders and ecotourists flock to immerse themselves in one of the most species-rich and biodiverse regions on the planet. In the northern region of Petén, the rainforest stretches unbroken for many miles of swamp and jungle.

Both the Caribbean and Pacific coasts have wonderful, palm tree-lined beaches with picture postcard-perfect tropical islands. If you like lots of action, throbbing music and exotic umbrella drinks with your beach, Guatemala has plenty of it. If you want a tropical island with white sand and coconut palms all to yourself, you can find that, too.

Food & Eating Out

One of the most wonderful reasons to visit Guatemala is to eat. The combination of wide international influence, fresh local produce and seafood and plenty of well-off business types and retirees willing to pay means the country has plenty of **truly great restaurants**.

Guatemala enjoys a wonderful cuisine combining colonial, Mayan, European, and Mexican flavors. Hotels and small restaurants offer a wide variety of steaks, chicken, seafood, pasta, rice and beans dishes and fabulous tropical fruits. A couple of the best **Guatemala City fine dining establishments** compare with the fanciest and tastiest of

STREET FOOD

Be sure to eat at **street stalls** whenever you can—fried chicken, tacos, ceviche are almost always wonderful. Everyone you meet has their favorite street food vendor. *You have to try the ceviche lady by the bank. I've been eating her ceviche for 15 years and I never got sick. It's great!* They always seem to add that part about never getting sick . . . . I have my own favorites. There's a guy who sells tacos in front of the school in Panajachel . . . .

any trendy big city restaurant in the world.

All the familiar North American fast food places are represented in Guatemala: McDonalds,

Burger King, Subway are all over the place. Local fast food fried chicken chain **Pollo Campero** can be found in almost every town.

Restaurant prices in Guatemala are similar to US prices in upscale restaurants but usually less in more modest places but the food is usually better in Guatemala. Restaurants tend to actually cook things rather than just heat up things. And the seafood and local fruits and vegetables are wonderful.

Be sure to try the local **típico** (traditional Guatemalan food) specialties. Some food choices will be similar to what you see in Mexican restaurants in the US. I love the **taquitos**, small tortillas filled with this or that deep fried and served with guacamole. The local, tiny tortillas are almost always patted into shape by hand and sometimes are made from blue corn.

RESTAURANT PRICES IN THIS BOOK

$: $5 or less/diner
$$: $5-8
$$$: $8-12
$$$$: $12-25
$$$$$: Over $25

Típico is savory and interesting based on local seafood, vegetables, and chicken. Small tortillas are typically served fresh three times a day. You will see ladies patting them up by hand, toasting them briefly on a hot *comal* and selling them to locals at *los tres tiempos*: breakfast, lunch and dinner. Rice, fried plantains, *plátanos*, are typical with breakfast. **Pipián**, a rich chicken stew with a sauce made of tomato and pumpkin seed is probably the best known traditional Guatemala dish and is delicious. Look for **pupusas, tamales, chuchitos**, and **paches**— variations of corn-stuffed or corn-enwrapped goodies. Guatemalans like to have a cup of coffee and a piece of sweet cake in the afternoon. You'll see lots of little shops selling cookies and sweet bread. Go for it.

I hope you like **chicken**. Guatemala is the chicken-eatingest place I have ever visited. The ever-present fast food chicken outlet, Pollo Campero, seems to be the favorite of everyone. Their restaurants are always clean and efficient and always packed with Guatemaltecos honking down the fried bird.

Smaller restaurants may have elaborate menus with seafood, various types of steaks, pasta, chicken and other appetizing items offered. Quite often, as you begin the ordering process, it comes to light that they actually don't have very many of the star attractions that feature on the menu. Each time you make another selection, the very polite waitress will tell you they don't have that today. When this happens, go for the chicken. They *always* have chicken.

Tourist restaurants charge much more than the places most locals eat in. You'll see many people buying full meals on the street from ladies carrying their entire restaurant in a basket on their head. Try this. I have been pleasantly surprised by the delicious, often unidentifiable stuff I've tried. Taco and fried chicken stands abound and are usually a good bet.

Shrimp, corvina (sea bass), **mojara** and **robalo** (snook) are good choices for local fish. I avoid mushy-textured tilapia wherever I go. **Black bass** is sometimes available in the Lake Atitlán area and is a very good eating fish.

Fruits to look for include delicious tiny, **sweet bananas, papayas, mangos, passion fruit, carambola, aguacate** and the weird but delicious **guanábana**.

A sad trend I have noticed is for some restaurants catering to middle class, upwardly-mobile Guatemalans to serve instant coffee instead of ground, Sunny Delight instead of fresh squeezed orange juice and toasted white bread instead of fresh tortillas. Some of these middle class *fresas* or yuppies scorn their roots and don't want to be seen consuming foods typically consumed by poor country people. Restaurants serving hot tortillas are either *comedores* aimed at poor working Guatemalans or rich gringo tourists—the middle class wants white bread.

Service, although almost always friendly or even enthusiastic, is **often much slower** than what you may be used to in the States. This is partly because they are actually cooking your food instead of nuking something. If you want to have your drink arrive before the meal, you will need to specify that very clearly. If you order a beer and a meal at the same time, you may well receive both at the same time— 30 or 40 minutes after you sat down and have been sitting at an empty table for all that time. At breakfast, coffee may arrive with the meal or even afterwards even though your head may be lying on the table and loud groans escaping from your caffeine-deficient body.

Restaurants are required by law to include a **12% tax** on the bill. Some don't do this. Sometimes this extra is mentioned on the menu and sometimes it comes as a surprise at the end of the meal.

Tipping is not standard and rarely runs over 10%. In a small *comedor*, you may round up your bill to the nearest even unit as a tip. Unlike Americans, most Guatemalans keep all their change from every transaction they make.

Drink

Guatemala is blessed with a couple of **good beers**, great rum and wonderful fruit juices to mix it with. Guatemala is home to the wonderful Ron Zacapa Centenario, internationally recognized as tasty and one of the best rums in the world.

The national drink is surely the ubiquitous **Gallo**, a rather thin,

Budweiser-like lager. Ask for *"una Gallo"*. Thinner, even more gaseous and with even less taste, is the also-very-popular **Brahva**. Other beers to look for are **Moza**, a dark, bock-type brew, **Cabro**, also light and **Monte Carlo**, thinner yet if possible. Beer is not particularly cheap in Guatemala. Regular 12 ounce bottles rarely

sell for under $1 in a bar and usually run in the area of $3. Bars sometimes serve beer in one liter bottles. You can buy these beauties in small shops, cold, for around $3. International beers like Bud, Heineken and Corona are more expensive.

Now we get to **rum**. Guatemala is home to the wonderful **Ron Zacapa Centenario**, internationally recognized as tasty and one of the best rums in the world. It's not cheap running about $40 for the 15-year-old stuff. Small shops sell a wide variety of other, cheaper interesting local and international rums. Try real Cuban **Havana Club**. You can't get it back home. Yum!

Wines from Spain, Chile, Argentina and increasingly, the US are served in most tourist-oriented restaurants and can be found in liquor stores. Prices are usually a little higher than what you may be familiar with paying in the US. Inexpensive, apparently locally-produced box wines are sold. **Clos** is one popular brand. Aficionados like to say "it's not really wine, but it's clos." You will run into this lovely stuff if you order house wines by the glass in some restaurants. It's not too bad, actually.

Lodging

Guatemala has a **wide array of hotels**: from remote five star luxurious jungle and beach lodges to big city business hotels with helipads and conference centers. From beachfront hippie havens to rock star hideaways, you will be sure to find accommodations to suit you. From under $10 per night to over $1,000 per night (per person) the range is extensive.

LODGING PRICES

$:	**$25 or less**
$$:	**$25-75**
$$$:	**$75-150**
$$$$:	**$150-300**
$$$$$:	**Over $300**

Prices in this book are for one double room per night for two people.

If you want to get close to nature but still have the comforts of luxury lodging and fine dining at the end of the day, Guatemala can accommodate you in almost all parts of the country. There is a wide variety of lodging, including wonderful rainforest lodges as well as big city business hotels. Surf camps, fishing lodges, birders' hideaways and beachfront romantic bungalows abound.

In most parts of the country, comfortable hotels are available at reasonable prices. With this plethora of choice, I suggest you take a little time and select places to stay that are full of character, out of the way, or interesting for some reason. If you must stay in a Sheraton, Westin or other multi-star big city business hotel you can find them in Guatemala City.

Posadas (inns), and **hospedajes** (hostels) are usually small hotels but sometimes the names are attached to large, luxury developments. You may also see clean-looking "auto hotels." These are actually hot sheet joints catering to locals by the hour, many of whom live in a large family with their parents, seeking an hour or two of intimate privacy. Notice most have garages for hiding your car.

Hotels are required by law to include a 22% tax on the bill. Some don't do this. Sometimes this is mentioned up front and sometimes it comes as a surprise at the end of your stay.

3. GUATEMALA CITY

HIGHLIGHTS

▲ Zone 10 – Zona Viva

▲ Palacio Nacional de La Cultura, Parque Central

▲ Museo Ixchel

▲ Great Eats, Live Music, Gambling

▲ Day Trip to Pacaya Volcano

INTRO

With a population of over four million, **Guatemala City** is huge, poor, and intimidating. The most up to date part of town, **Zone 10**, has international-quality restaurants and hotels and feels reason-

COORDINATES

Guatemala City, the capital of Guatemala, lies in a mountain valley in the south-central part of the country. The international airport is here, and the city is divided into 20 zones, of which **zones 1, 4, and 10** have the most hotels, restaurants, and tourist attractions.

ably safe and pleasant during the day. If you find yourself in town, there are a few things worth seeing, but **there are no world-class tourist sites** that you should worry about missing. Unless you are very comfortable traveling in third world countries, I suggest making an effort to spend as little time in Guatemala City as possible.

Guatemala City is the **second largest city in Central America** and, compared to other Central American capitals with the exception of Panama City, it is much cleaner with better infrastructure.

The **Centro Histórico, Zone 1**, used to be the center of town with all the banks, embassies, government and business offices. Little by

little these moved to the much more modern and, in many ways, more attractive Zone 10. What's left is hundreds of old buildings in an amazing collection of styles: colonial, neo-colonial, art deco, American and others. These wonderful old buildings are a little hard to appreciate since the area consists of fairly narrow streets jammed with smoke-belching buses with bald tires, trucks, taxis and thousands of honking cars. The sidewalks are lined with stalls selling everything from gum to guns. There is a staggering selection of bootleg CDs and DVDs.

Most of the buildings need maintenance. Some have collapsed in earthquakes and exist now as piles of rubble or as parking lots. I'm going to suggest that most of you **skip this part of town** except on a tour with a guide. If you are a seasoned Latin American traveler you will probably be able to appreciate this lively, slightly run-down part of town. There are a couple of good hotels. The **Palacio Nacional de La Cultura** has a fairly good museum.

Zone 10, or **Zona Viva**, is reminiscent of Miami or Panama City. High rise office buildings, banks, international-quality hotels, upscale restaurants and nightclubs proliferate. As such, there is really not much of interest but it is the best part of town to stay in for most visitors. Nearby **Zone 14** is an upscale neighborhood of gated communities with guards, razor wire and broken glass-topped walls and a pleasant, quiet atmosphere. Most of the embassies are located in this zone.

The rest of Guatemala City is to be avoided. Amazingly squalid slums surround the city.

 GUATEMALA CITY IN A DAY

If you find yourself in Guatemala City, use the opportunity to shop at the modern malls and sample the many fine restaurants. It's easy and cheap to get around by taxi— no need for buses or rental cars.

Morning
Shopping opportunities include two quite modern and complete malls. Both have a wide selection of US and international chain stores, such as **Sears** and **TGI Friday's**, as well as a few local shops.

There is an open-air artisans' market, **Mercado de Artesanías** on Boulevard Juan Pablo II near the airport that has a decent selection of tourist items. Bargain here. For fabrics and better-quality crafts, **In Nola** in Zone 10 is known for its extensive selection and high quality.

For the intrepid, the **Mercado Central** in Zone 1, near the National Palace offers a typical Central American urban fruit and vegetable (and everything else including donkeys) market experience. It's

SIGHTS

SIGHTS

Guatemala City

National Palace

1. Bodeguita del Centro
2. Hotel Otelito
3. Hacienda Real
4. Ciento Puertas
5. Cuatro Grados Norte
6. Westin Camino Real
7. Posada Belén

Zone 1

National Theatre

INGUAT

Olympic City

Zone 8

Bus Terminal

Zone 4

Zone 5

Torre

Zone 9

Museo Ixchel

Zone 10

Bulevar Liberación

Aurora International Airport

Los Proceres Mall

crowded and justly famous for inventive pickpockets.

If you simply must sightsee, I suggest hiring **local driver Raúl Rodasto** drive you around in his car. At only $12/hour he will take you around town showing you the sights and fight the traffic for you. He will be happy to wait for you as you shop, visit the market or other places of particular interest. He knows the good restaurants and can even set up an interesting evening of club-hopping if you are so inclined (and daring).

Info: Tel. 502-5775-8276.

Check out the weird **country relief map** thing in the sports complex **Parque Minerva**. It is a bit run down and kind of a puzzle to me why it exists at all but almost everyone you run into in the city will insist you need to see it. The large relief map does give you a very good feel for the topography of the country. All the mountains and rivers are there and you can climb towers to view the country from different angles. I'm glad I went but there is really not much else of particular touristic interest in Guatemala City anyway so you may as well check it out. Take a taxi.

STREET CRIME?

I enjoy some cities but I am not fond of Guatemala City. Most of the city is **third world rough**, which means **be careful and take taxis door-to-door at night**. Leave your passport (carry a photocopy) and most of your money and credit cards in your in room safe. DO NOT WEAR A FANNY PACK or one of those pouches around your neck things. Keep your cash in your front pocket. Have fun.

Afternoon

There are dozens of great places to eat lunch in town. For meat, **Rancho Hacienda** or **Parrillada Del Centro Histórico Dos Canelones** are both locals' favorites. The Rancho is a steak place usually stuffed with business

SIGHTS

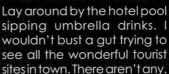

types choking down expense account lunches. It is a very well-run restaurant with top service. The Parrillada Del Centro is funky and plain with not much ambiance but great meat. Don't miss their *canelones*.

The **Museo Ixchel** displays traditional Mayan fabrics and their production. If you appreciate the intricate patterns of **huipiles**, and admire the colorful fabrics you see all over the country, this museum is a good stop to educate yourself on the variety of production techniques and different styles.

Spend the rest of the afternoon taking care of business or doing whatever errands brought you to Guatemala City in the first place. Then go back to your hotel for a rest.

Catch up on your sleep. At least you can eat very well in Guatemala City.

Evening
For dinner, **Jake's** and **Tamarindo's** are a couple of my favorites. They are both upscale, fine dining with good wine lists.

You can always find nightlife in Guatemala City. There are a few fairly laid-back live music places and plenty of loud, rowdy "nightclubs." I suggest you only visit these if you are big and strong, speak good Spanish and are comfortable running around third world cities late at night.

For live music lovers, **Bodeguita Del Centro** in Zone 1 is the place. The dark club has been the incubator for several of Guatemala's top bands and singer/songwriters.

A WEEKEND IN GUATEMALA CITY

SIGHTS

Although not a tourist destination by any stretch, Guatemala City has many interesting things to do and see. It is the commercial heart of the country. Guatemalans from rural areas and small villages come for shopping, business and to visit relatives. Tourists come to change planes.

GUATE!

Once you are in the country of Guatemala, Guatemala City is usually referred to as *"Guate"* or *"the City"* or *La Ciudad*. You will hear people saying things like: "I talked to my friend in the Guate yesterday" or "I'm going to *La Ciudad* next week."

Many international flights arrive in the afternoon, too late to transfer to most of the other parts of Guatemala and arrive before dark, so you may as well enjoy yourself and check out what the city has to offer.

Friday Evening

The International Airport is right in the middle of town. You can get a taxi from the airport to Zone 10 for only $5. Most of the better hotels will provide airport pickup service complete with a guy holding up a sign with your name on it just outside the arrivals hall.

I enjoy **Hotel Otelito** when I am in town. It is small, quiet and has a trendy bar and Asian restaurant. It is right in the middle of Zone 10 and in easy walking distance to most of the businesses you might need. It's only about a 10 minute ride to the airport. Reserve well in advance—they only have 12 rooms. After checking in, if it's not too late, walk two blocks for dinner at the wonderful **Rancho Hacienda** for steak and local side dishes. If it's after 8pm, take a taxi both ways.

There are a couple of good nightspots in town that are safe enough for tourists to go to. One of my favorites is the **Bodeguita del Centro**, which is a hip coffee house serving as an incubator for local bands. Several of the most famous Guatemalan rock bands were gestated here. It is a bit dark and gloomy but friendly and comfortable enough once you are in, sitting down and with a drink in your hand.

SIGHTS

Ciento Puertas is another downtown area with, guess what, 100 doors opening onto bars, music venues and funky restaurants. **Cuatro Grados Norte** is a newish entertainment district in the center of town with numerous live music venues.

Stop by the trendy bar at the hotel for a cocktail before shuffling off upstairs to your room for an early sleep.

Saturday Morning

There are a couple of marginal museums some may find to be of interest. Take taxis to these and unless you feel like wandering around in the slightly dodgy **Zone 1** looking for bootleg DVDs and knockoff purses, go back to the hotel afterwards. I suggest shopping after lunch.

But to start the day, taxi to Zone 1 for a look around. The imposing colonial and neoclassical former **Palacio Nacional de Cultura** (*photo on page 34 at bottom*) is located in the older part of town at the north end of the in the **Parque Central** (*photo below*). Since today's leaders prefer to live in more salubrious locations, it is now a museum. Free guided tours are offered. The place is rather run-down and sad.

The slightly better **Museo Nacional de Historia**, near the market features ancient documents, paint-

ings and a wonderful exhibit of 1875 photographs by Eadward Muybridge.

The **Museo Ixchel** displays traditional Mayan fabrics and their production. If you appreciate the intricate patterns of **huipiles**, and admire the colorful fabrics you see all over the country, this museum is a good stop to educate yourself on the variety of production techniques and different styles.

Saturday Afternoon
After Peruvian ceviche and other seafood for lunch at noisy **Ixtapa**, it's time to shop, shop, shop. Right?

Shopping is, as you might expect, extensive and varied. Check out the trendy shops in **Zone 10** or, for more downscale shopping, head to **Zone 1**, jammed with small kiosks selling absolutely everything. There are several large markets as well throughout town. See the *Shopping* section of this chapter for more details.

Saturday Night
For fine dining, **Jake's** is famous as one of the best eateries in Central America. I also

like **Tamarindo's**. Both are wonderful.

Some will want to explore Guatemala City's famous, slightly sleazy nightlife. **Gambling** is legal in Guatemala and there is a wide variety of places for visitors to indulge. Crummy bust out joints filled with dubious one-armed bandits vie with the only proper casino in the country: the aptly-named **Fantastic Casino** in Zone 10. The sort-of upscale gambling palace features a very few table games and about 150 slots. There are many other places but legally, they only have slots. Dubious ladies swarm tourists who venture into these fleshpots after dark. There are no top-quality venues like you would expect to encounter in Las Vegas.

Sunday
Day trips from Guatemala City are easily arranged through your hotel or one of the many tour agencies. Sunday is the most popular day to visit the colorful Mayan highlands market at **Chichicastenango**.

If you feel like climbing a volcano and watching lava

SIGHTS

and ash blast all over the place trips to **volcanoes Pacaya** (*see photo above*) and **Fuego** are easily arranged. If you leave early in the morning you can fly to Flores and visit the Mayan ruins of **Tikal** and fly back in time for dinner. Day trips to **Copán** by bus are a bit much for one day but can be arranged. Quaint and interesting **Antigua** is only an hour away and is easily explored and enjoyed as a day trip.

By now, day three, you have a good idea of any last minute purchases that need to be done. With luck, you have this down to just coffee and rum, and perhaps chocolate, all of which can be purchased at the airport. The airport is right in the middle of town, so unless the traffic is especially fierce, you can get there in a half hour or less from most parts of the city.

BEST SLEEPS & EATS

Guatemala City has a very good selection of hotels in all price categories. You can find clean, comfortable lodgings right in the city for as little as $50. There are a couple of international-quality business hotels sporting every conceivable hotel luxury and stylish, snappy boutique hotels coupled with trendy restaurants and hot nightspots.

Westin Camino Real $$$$
This is the nicest hotel in the country. Not the best. It has every conceivable convenience and is very new, modern and well-maintained. Inside the hotel, you are unable to determine whether you are in Los Angeles, New York or Panama. The only thing that gives the location away is the presence of candles and matches in the rooms. These are for use during the frequent blackouts. Soulless and plastic, it is the choice of well-moneyed gringos and business people from all over the world. I must reserve my "best of" designations for hotels with character and style. The Westin has neither although it offers just about every service and comfort any traveler could want. The restaurant is quite expensive but offers only mediocre food. They can cater to as many as 500 people at a time. There are wonderful places to eat only a block or so away. *Info: Avenida la Reforma y 14 Calle. www.westin.com; Tel. 502- 2333-3000.*

Posada Belén Museum Inn $$
Short on luxury but long on charm (and a real bargain at $30), the Belén is one of the most interesting hotels in the city. It is absolutely crammed with antiques and hundreds of pre-Columbian artifacts. The rooms are medium-sized and comfortable. The showers are adequate with hot water. There is no AC but you really don't need it. Upon request, the restaurant serves wonderful *típico*

meals. Service in the restaurant and the hotel are excellent. Perhaps the best things about the Belén are the fantastic owners. Rene and Francesca are wonderfully friendly and spend a large amount of time helping guests arrange tours, itineraries and transportation around the country. They have a nine-day itinerary that is particularly good. You could certainly feel good about having them arrange your entire visit to Guatemala. *Info*: *13 Calle "A" 10-30 Centro Histórico, Zona 1. www.posadabelen.com; Tel. 2253-4530.*

Hotel Pan American $$

Built in 1942 as one of Pan American Airline's flagship hotels around the world, the hotel retains quite a bit of its character although its charms are fading. The lobby features enormously high ceilings, period marble floors and very good quality Guatemalan huipiles and fabrics decorating the high walls. The lobby restaurant is ho-hum. There are great places to eat only a short taxi ride away. The place always seems to be packed with Guatemalan business people there for meetings in their large event facilities. The rooms are comfortable and well under $100.

BEST OF THE BEST IN GUATEMALA CITY

Otelito $$$

One of the best of the smaller hotels in town, the Otelito offers 12 rooms upstairs, behind the trendy, trendy, trendy bar and restaurant of the same name. You feel like you are staying in a private club. The rooms are large and comfortable. The  price is right and the location is in the best part of the city. They offer airport transportation services at odd hours. Their Wi-fi actually works in the rooms. This is one of my favorites for a quick overnight in Guatemala City. *Info*: *12 Calle 4-51 Zone 10. www.otelito.com; Tel. 502-2339-1811.*

This used to be a nice part of town and the area still has some charm but don't go out at night except by taxi. The quaint Rum Bar right by the front door is worth buying a drink in just to check out this old-time city hangout. *Info*: *9a Calle 5-63, Zone 1. Tel. 502-2232-6807.*

Biltmore Express Hotel $$$
The Biltmore is a good mid-price choice. It is centrally located in Zone 10 and is quite reasonably priced. It is part of the Camino Real complex, but cheaper. The entrance is on the other side of the block. A connecting door lets you access any of the Camino Real's services if you so desire. This is a fairly typical international business hotel, good for those who want the familiarity of a large western-style hotel without having to pay the price next door. It is a little on the plastic, sterile side but it's actually a good choice if you find yourself in town for a night and want something comfortable and easy. I find the desk staff to be very helpful arranging transportation and making reservations. Puzzlingly, their web site contains no contact information whatsoever. *Info: Zone 10, 15 Calle 0-31. www.caminoreal.com.gt; Tel. 502-2338-5000.*

Parrillada Del Centro Histórico Dos Canelones $$
For meat lovers, this is the spot. Large cuts of pork and beef are grilled over a wood fire and served with, actually not much else. You can order a salad but this place is all about meat. They are only open for lunch and until about 4:00. The place is popular with locals (you probably won't see any other gringos there) and they line up out onto the street at lunchtime. It's not at all fancy but the grilled meats are excellent. The fruit-filled *canelones* are wonderful. *Info*: Zone 1, 6 Avenida A.

Jake's $$$$
Jake's is an upscale French restaurant known all over Latin America for top quality fine dining. It is formal, elegant and offers a large menu with Italian and local specialties. Interestingly, one of the best eating fish in the sea, snook, is a featured menu item offered in 11 different preparations. They have a large selection of steaks and a $500 hamburger. The wine list is not huge but

SLEEPS & EATS

SLEEPS & EATS

THE LOUD ZONA!

As you walk through the **Zona Viva** in the evening, you will feel the sidewalk shake and your eardrums will pop due to the blast of extra-high volume music exploding out of every restaurant and bar you pass. Finding a quiet, intimate, tranquil bar or restaurant for a romantic evening is almost impossible. There are some exceptions. The expensive bars in the upscale hotels rarely blast their music. They blast out the latest football games on TV instead. I suggest the extremely expensive (but great) **Jake's** for a quiet meal.

offers a good selection of Chilean and Spanish wines. This is a safe, high end restaurant selection but I usually point people to Tamarindo's for the best fine dining in town. *Info*: *Zona 10, 17 Calle 10-40. www.grupoculinario.com/ jakes; Tel. 502 2368-0351.*

Hacienda Real $$$

This is a solid, properly-run businessman's steak house. It's large and busy and the food is great. A cup of soup arrives at your table almost the moment you sit down. They take great care of you, even bringing glowing braziers to your table to warm you up on cool nights. Ceviche and steak are good choices. The dining rooms are large with high ceilings with large booths and tables. The waiters are very professional. They have three locations. This one is in the nice part of town. *Info*: *Zone 10, 5a. Av. 14-67. Tel. 502-2380-8383.*

Tamarindos $$$

On Condé Nast's 2001 Hot List of the 100 most exciting new restaurants in the world, Tamarindo's is right up there with the trendiest New York eateries, but at half the price or less. I keep thinking this is an Italian restaurant but they "fuse" so many other cuisines, Thai, Mexican, Indonesian, and continental, into their menu that it is vastly more than just another Italian restaurant. Try their gnocchi—incredible. Try their moo shu duck and steak. They always have interesting daily specials. It is one of my favorites. Tamarindo's is very popular with wealthy Guatemalans. There are always several gigantic SUVs parked right in front with chauffeurs, bodyguards and other heavies hanging around. Walk right by all this. *Info*: *Zona 10, 11 Calle 2-19A, Zona 10, Tel. 502-2360-2815.*

Ixtapa $$$

Featuring Peruvian food, Ixtapa offers very good ceviche as well as reasonably good steaks. The menu offers several interesting seafood choices. The service is snappy. The ambiance = 0. Like many bars and restaurants in the area, they feel the need to have the music blasting at ear-splitting level at all times. The acoustics are terrible with tile floors, concrete walls and hard ceilings. The music is just a muddy roar. Be prepared for a (friendly) shouting session with your waiter to place your order. If you actually want to speak with your dinner companions, you will probably have to choose one of the more expensive, fine dining establishments like Jake's, where the music and noise level is slightly lower. *Info: Zone 10. Tel. 502-389-8956.*

BEST SHOPPING

Shopping in this city of perhaps four million inhabitants is, as you might expect, extensive and varied. There are plenty of **trendy shops in Zone 10** catering to wealthy locals and the few international visitors who venture into town. Most visitors will want to stay with the upscale shops in Zone 10. Bustling **Zone 1** is jammed with small kiosks selling absolutely everything. The streets seem barely passable as masses of traffic squeeze through the streets crowded with shoppers and hawkers. This is where to buy bootleg CDs, DVDs and cheap, knockoff Gucci, Fendi and Rolex.

The large and chaotic **Mercado Central** in Zone 1 near the palace is a large, indoor area with zillions of small stalls selling produce, meat, fabrics, used clothing, spices and other local and imported daily necessities as well as most tourist trinkets you will find all over the country. It is well-known for pickpockets, is crowded and dirty and not particularly quaint or

SHOPPING

colorful enough to warrant a visit from any other then the most intrepid travelers.

There is an open-air artisans' market, **Mercado de Artesanías** on Boulevard Juan Pablo II near the airport that has a decent selection of tourist items. Bargain here.

Several large, modern malls grace the city and all have the expected US and European luxury brands. The malls are bustling and the food courts jam-packed. These are good places to shop for cheap mobile phones and SIM cards. You will be comfortable with the likes of **Sears** and **TGI Friday's**.

For fabrics and better-quality crafts, **In Nola** is known for its extensive selection.

Info: *18 Calle 21-31*
Zone 10
Tel. 502-2367-2424

BEST NIGHTLIFE & ENTERTAINMENT

Guatemala City has plenty of late night partying, dancing, live music and happening casinos. Going out at night in town is not however, for the faint hearted. If being in a third world country freaks you out, stay in your hotel and watch TV. Seriously. If you do go out, have your hotel call a taxi to take you directly to your destination. Have the club or restaurant security people order you a cab directly back to your hotel when you are done. No lingering outside the club, no late night strolling around town peering into windows and reading restaurant menus.

Watering Holes
I like the little **Rum Bar** right by the front door of the Pan American hotel in Zone 1. It's from another, perhaps more colorful era and has a great selection of Caribbean and Central American rums.

Info: *9a Calle 5-63*
Zone 1

Casinos
Gambling is legal in Guatemala and there is a wide variety of places for visitors to indulge. Crummy bust out joints filled with dubious one-armed bandits vie with the only proper casino in the

NIGHTLIFE & ENTERTAINMENT

country: the aptly-named **Fantastic Casino**. The sort-of upscale gambling palace features a very few table games and about 150 slots.

Info: 14 Calle 2-51, Exterior Primer Nivel Hotel Intercontinental, Zona 10. Tel. 502-2379-8228.

There are many other places but legally, they only have slots. Dubious ladies swarm tourists who venture into these fleshpots after dark. There are no top-quality venues like you would expect in Las Vegas.

Prostitution
Prostitution is legal in Guatemala. Many tourists come to Guatemala specifically to meet willing Latinas for a short friendship. Nightclubs and casinos seem to be common places for a hookup, so don't be surprised if you're approached. What locals call "nightclubs" are usually what we in the US refer to as strip clubs.

Live Music Venues
There are numerous places to enjoy local and touring international musicians. **Bodeguita del Centro**, in the *Centro Histórico*, is well known as an incubator for local talent. **Ciento Puertas** is another downtown area with, guess what, 100 doors opening onto bars, music venues and funky restaurants. **Cuatro Grados Norte** is a newish entertainment district in the center with numerous live music venues.

BEST SPORTS & RECREATION

Most of Guatemala's activities can be done as **day trips** from Guatemala City. Most of the informative walks around town listed here for Antigua can be done as a day trip from Guatemala City. The ever-popular **hike up a volcano** to see lava heaving out is also an easy one. Such volcanoes are located conveniently right outside town.

Golf
In the last week of February, **San Isidro Golf Club** hosts the NGA/Hooters Pro Golf Tour. The course, in Zone 16, is about a 20-minute ride from the middle of Guatemala City and has a wonderful clubhouse, gym, squash courts and a modern, 18-hole course designed, presumably, by someone suitably famous.

SPORTS & RECREATION

WEAVING SCHOOL

If you really, really admire the local, astoundingly-bright local fabrics, you can schedule a weaving lesson with **Concepción Ratzán Mendoza**, *Tel. 502-7721-7409*. In three to six hours she can help you produce a 12" x 32" piece of colorful cloth hopefully resembling the beautiful things you see local women wearing and for sale in markets. The price for the lesson and materials is about $25.

Info: *Zone 16*
www.clubsanisidro.com
Tel. 502-2385-6524

Volcano Walks

Volcano climbs happen every day and leave from Panajachel, Antigua, Guatemala City and from some of the villages around Lake Atitlán. Some of the more spectacular climbs include the ever-spouting **Pacaya**. Some lava heads go so far as to spend the night on top of the volcano to better enjoy the sunrise. It gets cold up there. Other volcanoes may be quite a climb but yield little more than a meager view from a heavily-wooded peak. Ask your hotel to set something up for Pacaya or one of the other nearby peaks; the views are great and the trip is a lot of fun!

4. ANTIGUA

HIGHLIGHTS
▲ Cathedrals & Churches – impressive colonial buildings

▲ Walking Tour – history and architecture

▲ Day Trips – hike Pacaya Volcano and visit the market at Chichicastenango

▲ Parque Central – colorful colonial-era square with park, cathedral, shops and dining

SIGHTS

COORDINATES

Antigua is located an easy half-hour drive from the main international airport and lies at the base of the imposing **Agua volcano**. With its traditional *Parque Central*, it is compact and easy to enjoy on foot. Three volcanoes surround this beautiful old colonial city.

INTRO

Antigua is tops on just about every tourist's list of places to visit in Guatemala. It's easy to get to, it's picturesque, there are good hotels and interesting restaurants, the shopping is good and there is plenty of nightlife. The town is small, compact, and easily explored on foot. Students from all over the world here for Spanish language studies clog the streets adding a wonderful international mix to the scene. The awesome **Volcán Agua** looms ominously over the town. Puffs of smoke belch sporadically from **Volcán Fuego**, a little in the distance.

ANTIGUA IN A DAY

You can get a good feel for the town and see most of the more interesting sights in a day. The town is compact and easy to explore on foot. Shopping in small shops, cooperatives and at the handicrafts market is some of the best in Guatemala.

Morning
Start out in the middle of everything at the **Parque Central**. See the church, walk around, and grab a coffee. If you can, book a walking tour with **Elizabeth Bell**, noted historian and author. This is by far the best way to see and learn about the old churches, monasteries and assorted colonial ruins scattered spectacularly around town. You can certainly grab a map and walk around on your own but you're going to miss the stories, history and local color a personal guide provides.

Be sure to see the colorful and historic monasteries and churches. The impressive **Catedral de Santiago** faces

SIGHTS

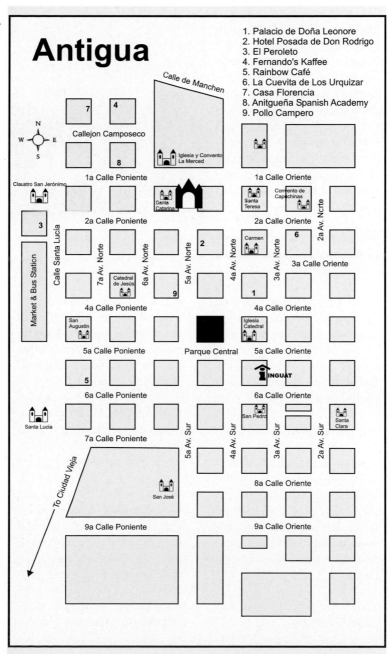

Antigua

Calle de Manchen

1. Palacio de Doña Leonore
2. Hotel Posada de Don Rodrigo
3. El Peroleto
4. Fernando's Kaffee
5. Rainbow Café
6. La Cuevita de Los Urquizar
7. Casa Florencia
8. Anitgueña Spanish Academy
9. Pollo Campero

SIGHTS

the Parque Central. If you go to the upstairs balcony of the **Palacio Del Ayuntamiento** across the street from the parque, you can get a great photograph of the Parque Central, Catedral de Santiago with the looming Agua volcano in the background. You can visit the incredible interior from a side entrance. No photos inside.

Next, be sure to see **Iglesia y Convento de Santa Clara** where Hermano Pedro worked his magic. His tomb is close by at **Iglesia de San Francisco.** His cult has grown over the years and hundreds of pilgrims still come to ask for his help. The **Iglesia y Hospital San Pedro** is now a charity hospital.

La Merced, Iglesia y Convento de Nuestra Señora de la Merced, is probably the most interesting and colorful of the churches in Antigua (*photo above right*). Pastel yellow with a fish fountain, there are good views from a balcony. No photos but visitors are welcome.

Info: *5 Avenida Norte and 1a Calle Poniente.*

For a mellow mid-morning snack, I suggest the peaceful courtyard of the **Sabe Rico** for a cup of great organic coffee or tea and some organic chocolate goodies.

I am sure you will keep an eye out as you walk around town for fabrics, handicrafts or artwork that appeals to you. I suggest using your morning walk to generally **scope out the shopping opportunities** and, after you have a good idea for what the town has to offer, go back in the afternoon to confirm those purchases you have been contemplating. A quick walk through the women's coop-

SIGHTS

erative **Nim Po't** just up from the arch at 5a Avenida Norte #29 will give you a good idea of what to expect in the smaller shops in town (*see more below*).

Afternoon
Lunch is ceviche at **El Peroleto** near the bus station. Try the mixed **ceviche with snails**. After lunch, shop, shop, shop and then stroll through the **handicrafts market** located near the bus station. It is fairly clean and not too crowded. Stall holders will definitely bargain with you. Cash works better than credit cards.

End up at **Nim Po't** just up from the arch at 5a Avenida Norte #29. The cooperative has a very good selection of fabrics and all the Guatemalan handicrafts you will probably be interested in. They don't have people annoyingly running around trying to get

ALTERNATE PLAN

Try the wonderful *típico* food on offer at **La Cueva de Los Urquizar**. They have a large, wood-fired stove in front with an array of bubbling pots you can pick your meal from. The staff is excellent about explaining the weird stews and strange salads. This is a very good stop.

SIGHTS

you to look at stuff. If you do need help, the ladies seem eager to answer questions. There are great piles of *huipiles* you can poke through on your own. Prices are marked and there is little bargaining. This way you can get a good idea of what the things you want to buy are worth. You can then go on through town shopping in galleries and small shops. At the end of the day you can always go back to Nim Po't and pick up the things you were not able to find elsewhere.

I particularly enjoy spending an hour or so walking in and out of **the galleries on 4a Calle Oriente**. The quality of the

SKIP THE CROSS

It seems like every tourist town has a few "must see" sites that are actually not particularly interesting but all the tourists go there anyway. The view of Antigua and surrounding volcanoes from **Cerro de La Cruz** is great but not worth the grueling climb up there. Security is also an issue on this excursion. The cross itself is a cross—much like many others you have probably already seen.

artwork is astounding. Some paintings by Ballesteros can sell for over $100,000. You can look at them for free.

Go by **Fernando's Kaffee** for fresh roasted coffee and a snack in the middle afternoon. They have a nice courtyard and wonderful fruit smoothies. They prepare fresh fruit juice to order, on the spot. They add no sugar, water, milk or anything else. Just fruit.

Walk aimlessly some more. Towards the end of the afternoon, you may stray towards a couple of Antigua's many interesting watering holes. **Frida's** Mexican restaurant right near the arch, next to Nim Po't has good bar snacks and drinks. Try also **Reilly's Pub** or the laid-back **El Muro** (*see Sleeps & Eats for more info*).

Evening
If you get to be in town for dinner, I suggest trying the beef bourguignon at the little **restaurant with no name** across the street from La Merced, 1a Calle Poniente. They only have a couple of tables but you can have a glass of wine at the bar while

you wait. It's worth it. This is a very informal place with wonderful food. The menu changes almost every day. This is not the restaurant on the corner. It is next door and has no sign. You can glance in the window as you walk by and check things out. Finding out about places like this is why you bought this book! When I have a free evening in Antigua I head immediately to the **Rainbow Cafe** for live music, poetry readings and open mike (Wednesday nights). **Riki's Bar** is also dependable for a lively bar scene and good music.

SIGHTS

A WEEKEND IN ANTIGUA

A weekend is plenty of time to wander around town checking out the shopping, visiting the churches and ruins of churches, and sampling the wonderful restaurants and nightlife.

Friday Evening
Check into the wonderful **Palacio de Doña Leonor** for a stay in the most luxurious and historical lodgings in the country. After refreshing, walk a half block to the **Parque Central** and take a slow stroll around the fountain (trying not to stare at the exposed, water-spouting breasts of the nymphs) and gawk at the **Catedral de Santiago**. Agua volcano looms over everything, setting the mood.

I generally like to walk around the fountain area once or twice seeing what the locals as well as tourist are up to and then circle the square again on the sidewalks, glancing into the tourist shops and restaurants just to get in the right frame of mind for dinner.

The magnificent **Catedral de Santiago** is on one side of the square. I like to go upstairs at the **Palacio Del Ayuntamiento** just across the street, where you can get a great photograph of the Parque Central and the Catedral de Santiago with the looming Agua volcano in the background. You can visit the interior of the church by a side entrance.

For just plain old good eats, very well prepared, try the hole in the wall restaurant with no name located just

SIGHTS

across the street from La Merced. With only a couple of tables and a few stools at the bar, this is one of my favorite restaurants in town.

Saturday Morning

Walking more or less aimlessly around Antigua is a great pleasure, but I recommend a guided walking tour if you would like to know more about the ruins and old stuff you are looking at. **Elizabeth Bell**, a noted historian and author, offers a great, very informative tour. Book well in advance. Even if you take a tour, I suggest grabbing a cheap map of the town from your hotel and spending almost all day on your own,

wandering into the shops, churches and restaurants that catch your fancy.

You will definitely want to see the **Iglesia y Convento de Santa Clara** where **Hermano Pedro** worked, hung out and did his laying-on-of-hands miracles. His cult has grown over the years and hundreds of pilgrims still come to ask for his help. If you thought that was fun, check out his tomb, close by at **Iglesia de San Francisco**. Hermano Pedro remains a popular figure all over Guatemala.

Also close by, the **Iglesia y Hospital San Pedro** is now a charity hospital. Probably the most interesting and colorful of the churches in Antigua, **Iglesia y Convento de Nuestra Señora de la Merced**, 5 Avenida Norte and 1a Calle Poniente, is pastel yellow with a fish fountain and good views from a balcony.

Many buildings in Antigua present a fairly bland, stucco exterior to the street with few, if any windows. As you walk around town, take opportunities to glance through open doorways and you will often see amazingly elegant courtyard gardens hidden from the street. Step into the **Hotel Posada de Don Rodrigo** and check out their amazing courtyard. Casual visitors are welcome. There are usually artists working in the garden and, in the afternoons, a típico marimba band rocks out.

Saturday Afternoon
After lunch, it's time for some serious shopping. I suggest parking any non-shopping members of your party at **Frida's** for an afternoon of margaritas, mojitos and nachos. The **handicrafts market** is located near the bus station and is fairly clean and not too crowded. Stall holders will definitely bargain with

ALTERNATE PLAN

Antigua is well placed for short day trips to **Volcán Pacaya**. Dozens of agencies can arrange a group trip to the base where you can buy walking sticks and hire horses for the long, two-steps-forward, one-step-back hike to the top, where you can see bubbling, flowing lava and such.

you. Cash works better than credit cards.

There are dozens of shops around town with fabrics and handicrafts. High prices and high quality typify some of the smaller shops on 5a Avenida Norte near Nim Po't

SIGHTS

SIGHTS

like **Nativo's** which has a very tasteful selection of fabrics mostly from cooperatives near Santiago de Atitlán. They have wall hangings, tablecloths, jewelry and purses. The prices are very high but the quality is usually a bit better than the other shops in town.

I like to do my shopping by browsing the small shops and craft markets without buying much and then go to Nim Po't to see if I can find any of the things I found in the other places for less money. A collective of a couple of dozen artisans, Nim Po't offers one of the largest selections of the kinds of fabrics, ceramics and "stuff" visitors to Guatemala are likely to want under one roof. They have a very good selection of **huipiles** arranged in piles sorted by price. You can poke through on your own until you find something you like. The sales attendants are helpful and not pushy. There is little if any bargaining going on and, I am told, the prices are fairly reasonable compared to what you might bargain for in a local market somewhere.

At this point it might be a good idea to go back to Frida's

and check on the by now, probably well-oiled non-shopping members of the group.

If you are sufficiently energized after coffee at Fernando's, do a little more exploring and then, once again, head for a comforting watering hole like **Café No Sé**. Well known mostly for an extensive selection of tequila and mescal, the atmosphere here will have you eating the worm in record time. They often have live music in the evenings.

Reilly's Pub is dependably full of expats young and old slurping down all sorts of good beer on tap (Guinness comes in a can. Sorry). It gets rowdy later in the evening. Very late, they lock the doors and the party inside just keeps on crankin'.

Saturday Evening
The restaurants around the Parque Central and on 5a Avenida Norte are good for people-watching but offer mostly medium-quality tourist fare. You can do much better for less money. That's why you bought this book.

SIGHTS

After dinner, as this is your last night in town, you have to go out and sample the famous nightlife. Antigua is swarming with young university students from all over the world and it is fun to rub shoulders with them and see what kind of music gets them up and dancing. Whenever I have a free evening in Antigua I like to go to the **Rainbow Café** for live music, poetry readings and open mike (Wednesday nights). It has a laid back university-student-hangout feel to it. It's rarely loud but usually packed and always friendly.

Other choices, if you are up for this sort of thing, are **La Casbah** and **La Sin Ventura**. La Casbah is a real-live 70s-era disco usually crammed with hip young types from Guatemala City hoping to charm the pants off the numerous student girls who flock there to dance, drink and meet hip young Guatemala City types. If salsa dancing gets you going, get going to La Sin Ventura. It's a little on the small side but the dancing and sounds are great. It's mostly a weekend place and can run late, late, late.

Sunday Morning
Even on Sunday, last minute shopping is possible. Most of the tourist-oriented shops will be open.

There's a variety of interesting day trips from Antigua. **Chichicastenango** is an easy one. Market days are Sunday and Thursday. Sunday is the busiest with the added spectacle of religious processions and ceremonies. You can get there and back in a day. Hikes to the top of **Volcán Pacaya** for lava sightings can either be a short day trip or an overnight, sunrise/lava viewing adventure.

Sunday Afternoon
Just outside town in Jocotenango is the wonderful **Centro Cultural La Azotea**. Some part of the large complex is bound to please everyone in your group. Three museums in one share the grounds. A full-on working coffee plantation and *beneficio* grows, processes and ships organic coffee. On the same premises are an extensive museum of traditional Guatemalan musical instruments and a large display of traditional Mayan clothing.

SIGHTS

The smart young lady who led my tour seemed to be able to play all the instruments at least a little and was quite informative about the clothing and coffee production. I generally avoid these types of tourist "attractions," but I really enjoyed my afternoon visit to the Centro Cultural La Azotea.

Sunday Evening
It is usually less than an hour ride back to Guatemala City from Antigua so, as long as you're not the one driving, you can put off your return as late as possible and cram down yet another wonderful meal.

A WEEK IN & AROUND ANTIGUA

Lots of people come to Antigua for a week, two weeks and even more. One of the attractions is the huge number of **Spanish language schools** catering to students and casual tourists from around the world. The quaint town itself and the beautiful surrounding area offer numerous attractions and activities.

Sign up for a week of one-on-one Spanish classes for four hours every morning—a real bargain for around $5 per hour for one-on-one instruction. Explore the town on foot and visit the nearby attractions in the afternoon. In the evenings, sample Antigua's many wonderful restaurants and participate in its thriving night life. On Sunday, take a day trip to the colorful highland market at **Chichicastenango**.

Parque Central
The first thing to do for most visitors and a good way to get the flavor of Antigua is to take a stroll around the **Parque Central**. If you can, keep your eyes off the fountain in the center, or perhaps have your picture taken with the nymphs spouting water from their breasts. The magnificent **Catedral de Santiago** is on one side of the square. I like to go upstairs at the Palacio Del Ayuntamiento just across the street where you can get a great photograph of the Parque Central and the Catedral de Santiago with the looming Agua volcano in the background. You can visit the

interior of the church by a side entrance.

One of the best things about Antigua is the wide variety of excellent restaurants. I try to avoid the overtouristed places around the Parque Central and can point you to less-touristed places for wonderful lunches, dinners and afternoon snacks in less crowded venues.

I suggest you spend your first day in town simply wandering around soaking in the sights and marveling at the huge volcano that looms over everything. Grab a cheap tourist map from your hotel to orient yourself and locate any "must see" sites.

Right by the Parque Central, if you are up for this sort of thing—dancing and very loud music that is—**La Casbah** is a real-live 70s-era disco usually crammed with hip young types from Guatemala City hoping to charm the pants off the numerous student girls who flock there to dance, drink and meet hip young Guatemala City types. The obligatory mirrored disco ball rotates from the ceiling. Cool.

Walking Tours

If you are interested in learning more about the history of what you are looking at, a walking tour with noted historian **Elizabeth Bell** is a great way to begin your explorations of Antigua. Her tours take in the main churches (and ruins of churches), parks, elaborate haciendas and include a historical and cultural talk with plenty of room for questions and stories. Most walks last about three hours.

Hotel Posada de Don Rodrigo

Many buildings in Antigua present a fairly bland, stucco exterior to the street with few if any windows. As you walk

SIGHTS

ALTERNATE PLAN

If you are going to be studying Spanish for the week at one of the local Spanish language schools, consider going for a **home stay with a local family**. This economical option adds to the "total immersion" learning experience. Home stays usually include private rooms and meals.

around town, take opportunities to glance through open doorways and you will often see amazingly elegant courtyard gardens hidden from the street. Step into the **Hotel Posada de Don Rodrigo** and check out their amazing courtyard. Casual visitors are welcome. There are usually artists working in the garden and, in the afternoons, a típico marimba band rocks out. This is a great example of Colonial Spanish architecture at its best.

Exploringing the Old Churches

I suggest an informal afternoon walk to visit some of the interesting churches in town. You will definitely want to see the **Iglesia y Convento de Santa Clara**, where **Hermano Pedro** (Brother Peter) worked, hung out and did his laying-on-of-hands miracles. His cult has grown over the years and hundreds of pilgrims still come to ask for his help. If you thought that was fun, visit his tomb, close by at **Iglesia de San Francisco**. Hermano Pedro remains a popular figure all over Guatemala.

Also close by, the **Iglesia y Hospital San Pedro** is now a charity hospital. Probably the most interesting and colorful of the churches in Antigua, **Iglesia y Convento de Nuestra Señora de la Merced**, 5 Avenida Norte and 1a Calle Poniente, is pastel yellow with a fish fountain and good views from a balcony.

Handicrafts Market

The **handicrafts market, Mercado de Artesanías**, is located near the **bus station** and is fairly clean and not too crowded. It's a good place to browse, but be prepared to bargain. Stall holders definitely expect to bargain with you. Cash works better than credit cards. Most of the things tourists are looking for, masks, huipiles, and fabrics are in the stalls. If you feel comfortable with your knowledge of what things sell for, by all means start haggling.

Info: 4ª Calle Poniente Final.

Nearby is the colorful **bus station**. You can walk through the bustling dirt parking area marveling at the elaborately decorated "chicken buses."

Touts will try to get you to take their particular bus to destinations all over Guatemala and Central America. Bring your camera for some great shots of the colorful buses.

Centro Cultural La Azotea
I enjoyed my afternoon trip to the coffee beneficio/musical instrument/folklore museum, **Centro Cultural La Azotea,** just outside town at Jocotenango. It is a cheesy tourist attraction but well done. I always like tours of anything to do with coffee production. The instrument museum is large and the staff seems to be able to play all the instruments. Cool. Three museums in one share the

grounds. A full-on working coffee plantation and *beneficio* grows, processes and ships organic coffee. On the same premises are an extensive museum of traditional Guatemalan musical instruments and a large display of traditional Mayan clothing. The smart young lady who led my tour seemed to be able to play all the instruments at least a little, and was quite informative about the clothing and coffee production. I generally avoid these types of tourist "attractions" but really enjoyed my afternoon visit to the Centro Cultural La Azotea.

Macadamia Nut Farm
A short, 15 minutes bus ride outside Antigua, the **Valhalla Macadamia Nut Farm** is a working macadamia nut farm open to the public with an English- and Spanish-language tour explaining the macadamia nut production in general and the story of the farm itself. If you are a macadamia nut yourself, you will enjoy the small shop selling nuts, nut butter and other macadamia products including facial creams.

Volcán Pacaya
Antigua is well placed for short

SIGHTS

day trips to **Volcán Pacaya** (*photo above*). Dozens of agencies can arrange a group trip to the base where you can buy walking sticks and hire horses for the long, two-steps-forward, two-steps-back hike to the top, where you can see bubbling, flowing lava and such. Hardcore hikers take late afternoon trips and spend the night. The idea is that the energetic matrix will be especially strong at sunrise. So your pictures will come out better. Or something.

Elizabeth Bell arranges one of the best tours to **Volcán Pacaya**. She is known for running top-quality vehicles with friendly, English-speaking guides and drivers. Volcano hikes are easy to arrange for half day, full day or even overnight. It's cold on top so dress warm.

Chichicastenango
Another good side trip from Antigua is a half or full day trip to **Chichicastenango** for the colorful market and extravagant church activities. It's only a couple of hours by tourist shuttle van, and is a great day out. Famous as the most interesting and colorful village market in Central America, Chichi is a must for all tourists. For me, it is a little too busy for comfortable shopping, but the sheer spectacle of the market and the adjacent church activities bring me back over and over again.

Sunday is perhaps the best day to visit the market and churches. Thursday is also market day at Chichi but the religious processions and other church activities are not

on. The market is less crowded then, but not quite as interesting.

Shuttle vans can be arranged to take you from your hotel in Antigua directly to the market at Chichicastenango. They usually leave in the morning at 10am and return in the afternoon around 4pm. The shuttles park near the action and usually return after about 4 hours at the market.

lections and a less high-pressure shopping atmosphere.

All the popular tourist things are for sale here. If you already have a good idea of what you want and more or less how much it should cost, then Chichi may be a good place to make your final purchases. If the chaotic market atmosphere suits you, you may enjoy jamming your way through the crowds and bargaining at small market stalls. The selections at the market

in Chichi can be quite good for some items, but both Antigua and Panajachel may have better se-

One of the nicest things about a visit to Chichi is the opportunity to take photographs of the colorful locals a little bit easier than in other locations. The crowd is large and there are seemingly hundreds of other gringos holding cameras out in front of them taking shots of colorful Mayan women and exotic-looking market stalls. I like to sit on the church steps slightly above the crowd level and casually snap telephoto shots of the action. The colorful religious processions, held on Sundays, are one of the most photographed events in Guatemala.

SLEEPS & EATS

BEST SLEEPS & EATS

There are dozens and dozens of hotels, lodges and inns in Antigua. Prices range from $5 for backpacker dorms to hundreds per night for stylish, upscale digs. Many are dripping with charm and local color. For those who must have all the features of the big name international hotels, a Camino Real is planned.

BEST OF THE BEST IN ANTIGUA – MY FAVORITE HOTEL IN GUATEMALA!

Palacio de Doña Leonor $$$$

This is a real jewel of a boutique hotel. It was built in the 16th century for Doña Leonor, the daughter of conquistador Don Pedro de Alvarado and a Tlaxcalan Indian princess, Tecuilhuatzin. He forcefully took her for his wife, as spoil of the conquest when he conquered the area but the marriage turned out to be a happy one. The entire building has been lovingly restored to near its original, colonial condition. It is loaded, loaded, loaded with charm. The 12 rooms and suites are arranged on the upper level surrounding the traditional interior courtyard, which is crammed with orchids, bromeliads and other exotic flowers and plants. A pool, spa, gym and restaurant are planned for the near future. It is only a half block from the central plaza—a wonderful location.

Each room is unique. Many rooms have their own fireplace. The beds are made with excellent linen and the bathrooms come with organic artisanal toiletries. Delightful nighttime treats are

delivered to your door. Art and antiques litter the rooms and halls. Their wi-fi service, as in most hotels these days, works sort of okay. The hotel is owned by the same family that owns the beautiful Hotel Atitlán in Panajachel. Guests include visiting diplomats, royalty and dignitaries. The tea room/bar is quite the thing, relaxing and comfortable. They offer a choice of about 20 types of loose tea, and complimentary iced hibiscus tea all afternoon.

This is a class act. *Info: 4a Calle Oriente 8. www.palaciodeleonor.net; Tel. 502-7832-2281.*

Posada De Don Rodrigo $$$

The Posada seems like a hidden oasis right in the middle of town. The rooms surround pleasant courtyards with tinkling fountains,

live marimba music and views of the volcano. It's all very quaint, with furniture and *objets d'art* in period style. The rooms are pleasant and well appointed. Some rooms are a bit dark. It's a pretty big place, so you may be able to pick and choose a bit when selecting your rooms. The restaurant is quite nice with wonderful service, if a bit touristy, with a great volcano view. The hotel is located right on Avenida 5a close to all the main attractions of Antigua. *Info: Avenida 5a #22. www.posadadedonrodrigo.com; Tel. 502-7832-9858.*

Casa Florencia Hotel $$

This is one of the better bargains in town. The rooms are attractive and comfortable arranged around the side of a courtyard. They are provided with fans, TVs and safes. There is a nice view of Agua Volcano and pleasant plantings in the small garden area.

The large breakfast (Sundays only) includes the usual fruit, interesting breads and rolls, cereal, juices and coffee. Guests can use the lobby PC for internet access. *Info: 7 Avenida Norte #100. www.cflorencia.net; Tel. 502-7832-0261.*

Posada Del Angel $$
If it was good enough for Bill Clinton, it is good enough for me. With a total of seven rooms and suites, Posada Del Angel earns top ratings for small, boutique hotels in Antigua. There is a small pool, but, overall, a very quiet ambiance. The new owners' policies attract a mix of honeymooners, discreet business types, diplomats, the Prince of Saxony and the like. *Info: 4a. Avenida Sur #24a. www.posadadelangel.com; Tel. 502-7832-0260.*

DINING OUT IN ANTIGUA

Antigua has the best selection of interesting restaurants in the country. However, you need to avoid the most convenient and attractive tourist joints on or near the Central Plaza. Trust this guide implicitly. I have spent countless evenings choking down tourist fare in far too many Antigüeña restaurants. I present here only the pick of the crop.

My favorite eatery in Antigua is a two-table hole in the wall that doesn't even have a name. Because of the large, college-age tourist population, there are dozens of places offering pizza, frozen yogurt, burgers, Thai food. Most of them are not worth the time. Some like to sample the local cuisine in *típico* restaurants (a good idea) while many tourists want to hang out where the other tourists hang out: pubs, sports bars, rum bars, tequila bars, karaoke bars and, of course, McDonald's and Burger King.

If you want to sample local, *típico* dishes, you will have a hard time finding anything really *auténtico*. Don't get me wrong, there are several good *típico* places, but you must realize that in this tourist town, their primary clientele is tourists. So relax, accept the fact that you are a gringo tourist, you always will be, and enjoy yourself.

BEST OF THE BEST RESTAURANTS

Restaurante Don Martin $$$
I suppose I should call the food here high-end Guatemalan fusion but, although the food is delicious, I'm not sure what they are fusing it with. The room is nicely decorated with interesting local art highlighted on minimalist, stark white stucco walls. I had an edible eggplant ceviche served with blue corn tortilla chips, followed by a quite nice chicken breast with a sauce made from *green* tomatoes, *green* peppers and *green* onions, served with miniature vegetables and blue corn tortillas. Very festive. If you don't spend too heavily on wine, the price for dinner here is actually a bit less than at some of the more predictable, more touristed places closer to the central square. They serve dinner every day except Monday, and also serve a nice lunch on Sunday afternoons. *Info:* 4 Avenida Norte #. 27. Tel. 502-7832-2925.

Café Mediterráneo $$$
Mysteriously, many people recommend this dive. They have good food but rude service, and they are overpriced. The room is lacking any sort of charm whatsoever, unless you count a leaky roof as "charming." This is a menu-on-the-blackboard kind of a place. I am told a real Italian lurks in the kitchen preparing fresh pasta every day. I found the pasta dishes to be simple and delicious. A small salad, bowl of pasta (no meat) and two disappointingly small glasses of house wine set me back $40. Normally, I would not mention a place like this—my editor likes for me to write about only the best places—but several hotel owners recommended it to me and I thought I should set the record straight. Blow this one off. If, like me, you like a good Italian meal a couple of times a week, wait until you get to Panajachel and visit the wonderful Chez Alex for the real thing. *Info: 6a Calle #6.*

Restaurante del Arco $$
The food here is nothing special, but the dining area is located in the courtyard of an old convent, and you can see the cells the nuns used to inhabit. Expect the usual sandwiches, steaks, pasta, chicken and seafood. *Info: Antigua, 5a Avenida Norte.*

Frida's $$

Very good Mexican food and a great bar (¡mojitos!). Everyone raves about the quesadillas. Get a seat in the front smoking section, since the rear, non-smoking section near the bathrooms smells like piss. Otherwise, I like the place. It seems to attract the sort of North Americans who have just been fishing for marlin for several days. You can tell by their shirts and drinking habits. *Info: 5a Avenida Norte #29. Tel. 502-7832-0504.*

Tartins $$

This is a nice little restaurant a half block from the central plaza, across the street from the Palacio de Doña Leonor. The menu is not large but the daily specials are usually of interest. Panini, seafood and more or less local dishes are served with Italian flair. They only have two tables downstairs, with several more up a circular staircase. Try to get the table in front by the door—you can enjoy watching the parade go by on the street while you eat. *Info: 4a Calle Oriente.*

Fernando's Kaffee $$

This is a great, bohemian-style coffee spot. It's just around the corner from the **Catedral Merced**. The doorway is almost blocked by a funky-looking coffee roaster, which is usually in action. Push on by, as there is a large courtyard in back where you can enjoy their wonderful coffee, breakfasts, lunches, and fresh fruit smoothies. It is a good place to buy coffee to take back home. They also have interesting craft chocolates on hand. *Info: 7 Avenida Norte 43.*

Cuevita de las Urquizas $$

If you want to sample *típico* Guatemalan or traditional Mayan foods, you don't really have many options, but La Cuevita is about as good a shot as you are ever going to get. It's a good choice. There are a couple of dozen pots full of interesting-smelling things bubbling away on a stove up front by the entrance. You get to walk right by all the cooking food and you make your selection as you come in. If you have trouble communicating with the cook, you can just point to things that look good and he'll lift up a full ladle for you to peruse more closely. All the mysterious things I've tried here have been good. Go for it. *Info: 2a Calle Oriente 9D.*

La Taquiza $$

This is a nice quiet spot for fajitas, taquitos, flautas, and other Guatemalan/Mexican plates. They have a selection of vegetarian bits and pieces. It's a small courtyard place with only four or five tables but they have draft beer available by the glass or in pitchers. Nice! *Info: 3 Calle Poniente No. 14 D. Tel. 502-5693-0111.*

Sabe Rico $$

Antigua is full of places that look very ordinary from the outside but open up into quiet, fragrant, interior courtyards. Sabe Rico has tables widely scattered through their courtyard herb garden. It is very peaceful and a wonderful place to get away from the street crowds and noise. The gringo owners offer an interesting take on traditional Guatemalan foods, with a good selection of organic vegetarian plates and meaty entrees. They do chocolate. I once spent a wonderful afternoon here drinking beer and letting the waiters bring us snacks they selected for us to try from time to time. Great! *Info: 6 Avenida Sur #7. Tel. 502-7832-0648.*

Las Palmas $$$

Las Palmas has the reputation for being one of the "better" restaurants in town. It is regularly busy with tourists sampling the usual chicken, beef and fish entrees offered all over town, but prepared and presented a little nicer than at most of the other places. The ambiance is high colonial style with nice local artwork on the walls. They have a decent but expensive wine selection. Service is attentive and friendly. *Info: 6a Avenida Norte #14. www.laspalmasantigua.com; Tel. 502-7832-0376.*

Place with No Name $$

If you get to be in town for dinner, I suggest trying the **beef bourguignon** at the little restaurant (it has no name) across the street from La Merced. They only have a couple of tables, but you can have a glass of wine at the bar while you wait. It's worth it.

This is a very informal place with wonderful food. The menu changes almost every day. This is not the restaurant on the corner. It is next door and has no sign. You can glance in the window as you walk by and check things out. Finding out about places like this is why you bought this book. *Info: Across the street from La Merced next door to the restaurant on the corner, 1a Calle Poniente. They do not have a sign.*

Sangre $$$

In back of a high-end gift shop, Sangre has the best wine selection in town. They offer over 30 wines by the glass. Not cheap, but good. The setting is Guatemalan trendy, with an effort towards stark glass and stainless steel. It comes off as comfortable and inviting. The food is inventively prepared and lavishly presented, and runs along the lines of chicken satay, figs stuffed with interesting cheeses and garlic shrimp. Portions are smallish, the idea being that you will order several dishes (*bocas*) and share them. *Info: 5a Avenida Norte.*

La Fonda De La Calle Real $$$

This place has lots of *típico* selections, but the great location makes it a little over touristed. Good, though. Try the *rellenos*. **La Fonda de La Vuelta** at 3a Calle Poniente No. 7. (Tel. 502-832-0507) is another branch with pretty much the same things on offer. *Info: 5a Avenida Norte No. 5. Tel. 502-832-2696.*

El Peroleto $$

Ceviche is what this Salvadoran-owned restaurant is all about. It is right near the bus station and crafts market, and is my favorite lunch option in Antigua. Ceviche comes in several sizes and varieties: shrimp, fish, snail and combinations. I find the small size is almost more than I can handle. Try it with salsa inglesa. Very good! *Info: 7A Calle Poniente #34.*

BEST SHOPPING

Antigua is by far the best place to shop for Guatemalan crafts, textiles and fine art. There are dozens of shops to choose from. **Nim Po't** offers an enormous selection of the basic tourist purchases at fair prices in a comfortable setting. The very best quality artwork is found in the small galleries along Calle 4a Oriente. Some of the finest art in Central America is on display with some works of prominent artist Ballesteros going for over $100,000.

By the bus station is a largish "crafts" or "artisans'" market, the **Mercado de Artesanías**. **Info**: *4ª Calle Poniente Final*. There are dozens of small stalls selling fabrics, ceramics, wild masks, etc. Bargaining is expected but don't expect to buy anything particularly cheaply. Vendors will usually take credit cards here but want to up the price by as much as 10% for the privilege. If you are looking for simple ceramics, be sure to check out what is on offer in the nearby fruit and vegetable market.

Antigua is one of the best places in Guatemala to shop for traditional fabrics, handicrafts, ceramics and jewelry. There are hundreds of shops and small stalls. If you have a couple of days in town, I suggest you don't get in too big a hurry to make your purchases. I find the large and friendly **Nim Po't** is where I end up buying most of my stuff anyway, so I try to swing by on the first day or so after arriving in town just to get a feel for prices and the types of things I might want to buy in this trip. Their selection is huge and, since they are a fixed-priced cooperative, the ladies staffing the place don't really hassle you. You can take your time and poke through big piles of **huipiles** or whatever as you please. As I walk around town I pop into shops whenever I see some-

SHOPPING

thing that catches my eye and, near the end of my stay, I go back to Nim Po't to compare prices, quality, etc. There are a couple of smaller shops nearby that have quite high-quality things with correspondingly higher prices.

La Antigua Galería del Arte
This is by far the nicest gallery in town. Featuring prominent Latin American artists like Virginia Tagle, Ballesteros and others, this is a fantastic place to spend an hour or so in browsing around with your hands in your pockets wishing you were rich(er).

Info: 4A Calle Orient #15. www.artintheamericas.com; Tel. 502-7832-2124.

Jade is mined in several parts of Guatemala, and no visit to Antigua would be complete without a trip to a jade factory with the opportunity to buy the stuff as well. There are numerous places to buy jade. The largest and nicest is **La Casa de Jade**.

Info: 4a Calle Oriente No. 10 and El Reino del Jade Info: 5 Avenida Norte, just down from the arch).

It's difficult to avoid a tour of one of the jade factories. I find the factories and the stores to be mildly interesting.

Casa de Artes
Casa de Artes is much pricier and smaller than Nim Po't, but I find the quality here to be very good. Their selection of **Mayan textiles**, **wooden figures**, **ethnic jewelry** and **Majolica ceramics** is fairly limited, but they tend to have only the best examples. They have a nice selection of extremely expensive ceremonial masks. Visit their web site to get an idea of the types of things they offer.

Info: 4 Avenida Sur # 11. www.casadeartes.com; Tel. 502-7832-0792.

Nativos
Just about next door to Nim Po't, Nativo's has a tasteful selection of fabrics, mostly from cooperatives near Santiago de Atitlán: **wall hangings, tablecloths, jewelry and purses**. The prices are very high but the quality here is usually a bit better than at the other shops in town.

Info: 5a Avenida Norte #25B. Tel. 502-7832-6556.

Nim Po't

A collective of a couple of dozen artisans, Nim Po't offers one of the largest selections of the kinds of fabrics, ceramics and "stuff" visitors to Guatemala are likely to want under one roof. They have a very good selection of **huipiles** arranged in piles sorted by price. You can poke through on your own until you find something you like. The sales attendants are helpful and not pushy. There is little if any bargaining going on and, I am told, the prices are fairly reasonable compared to what you might bargain for in a local market somewhere. They have a good selection of postcards. The high-priced, superior-quality merchandise tends to be found in the smaller, trendy stores around town but Nim Po't is a good place to buy presents and get an idea of what crafts and textiles may cost as you go around the country.

Info: 5a Avenida Norte # 29. Tel. 502-7832-2681.

Buy your fresh-roasted coffee and craft chocolates at **Fernando's Kaffee**.

Info: 7 Avenida Norte 43.

BEST NIGHTLIFE & ENTERTAINMENT

Antigua is a great place to enjoy yourself in the evening. Due to the hundreds of students always packing the town, there are hundreds of bars, clubs, dance spots and laid back student hang-around places to pick from. Most students come to Antigua for three reasons: to have fun, to have fun, and to study Spanish. Bless 'em.

Watering Holes
El Muro
"The Wall" is comfortable and a little funky, with beat-up couches and lounge chairs and a nice, quiet vibe. Lots of the usual students and expats come for reasonably-priced beer and bar snacks.

Info: 3a Calle Oriente #19. Tel. 502-7832-8849.

Frida's
These guys have good drinks, great nachos and fine Mexicanish food in general. Too bad about the smell in

the back near the bathrooms though.

Info: 5a Avenida Norte #29. www.vivafrudas.com; Tel. 502-7832-0504.

Riki's Bar

Waaay too loud and noisy for anyone who is not in the mood, Riki's caters to students and international party types. I suggest avoiding the 7-9pm happy hour, but they do have very good quality live music almost every night. This is really the only place in town with a large room dedicated just to live music.

Info: 4a Avenida Norte #4. Tel. 502-7832-1327.

Café No Sé

Well known mostly for an extensive selection of tequila and mescal, the atmosphere here will have you eating the worm in record time. They occasionally have live music. This is one of my favorites.

Info: 1a Avenida Sur #7. Tel. 502-5501-2680.

Reilly's Pub

This is more or less a pub, and usually crowded with students and expats propping up the bar. You can order fish and chips but the Guinness comes in a can. Things can get very crowded late at night. The place is often "heaving".

Info: 5a Avenida Norte #31. Tel. 502-5672-7910.

Nightclubs

A "nightclub" in Guatemala usually means what North Americans call a "strip club," with pole dancers, lap dances and the like.

Mono Loco

I'm not sure you should actually Mono Loco a "nightclub" but it has sports on TV downstairs and a large rooftop guzzling area. The main part of the club has concrete walls, concrete floor and concrete ceiling, adding an acoustic challenge to the intersex mingling that attempts to happen here. It's too loud for me, with no pleasant ambiance other than lots of gringas who obviously have a different opinion about the place than I do.

Info: 5a Avenida Sur #6.

Live Music Venues
There are half a dozen places in town offering regular live music, and many others with the occasional live band or single act on the weekends. The restaurant at the **Hotel Panza Verde** has quiet, restaurant-style live music every night including an excellent Cuban group. Restaurant **Las Palmas** has similar dinnertime entertainment.

Rainbow Café
Very popular with gringo students, The Rainbow is almost always packed in the evenings for entertainment as diverse as poetry readings, flamenco guitar, straight-ahead rock acts and lots of what I call "Latin singer-songwriter" acts. I love the place and, if I am in town, will absolutely not pass up being on hand for their Wednesday night *micrófono abierto* (open mike).

Info: 7a Avenida Sur #8. www.rainbowcafeantigua.com; Tel. 502-7832-1919.

Café Sky
Famous for its great views from the rooftop lounge area. This is one of the more popular bars in town with the international student cluster.

Info: corner of 1a Avenida and 6a Calle. Tel. 502-7832-7300.

Dance Clubs
Even though all the thousands of students in town spend their evenings quietly in their rooms studying their irregular Spanish verbs, Antigua manages a lively dance scene.

La Casbah
This is a real live 70s-era disco, usually crammed with hip young types from Guatemala City hoping to charm the pants off the numerous student girls who flock to dance, drink and meet hip young Guatemala City types.

Info: 5a Avenida Norte #30. Tel. 502-7832-2640.

NIGHTLIFE & ENTERTAINMENT

La Sin Ventura

For satisfying your lust for the latest Latin dancing crazes, La Sin Ventura is all about dancing—salsa and the latest offshoots. It's a little on the small side but the dancing and sounds are great. It's mostly a weekend place and can run late, late, late. Classes for beginners to advanced students are available.

Info: 5a Avenida Sur #8. Tel. 502-7832-0581.

BEST SPANISH LANGUAGE SCHOOLS

It's a great idea to sign up in advance for a week of one-on-one Spanish classes in the morning or afternoon. No matter what level linguist you are, even a beginner, you will benefit enormously from spending a few hours formally studying the language of the country you are in. This is a great way to make yourself more comfortable interacting with people you meet.

Whenever I visit Guatemala, I start off my trip with a week of studying Spanish just to get myself in the mood and sharpen my ears. I like to learn some new localisms and catch up on the latest slang. The teachers are real pros and know which things gringos usually get wrong and which things they need to learn first.

There are over 100 registered Spanish language schools in Antigua. I have studied several times at the **Academia Antigüeña** and have visited and spent time at several others. These are serious schools, well run and staffed with university graduates trained in teaching Spanish as a second language to gringo tourists, like us. A few schools teach some Mayan languages as well as Spanish. The schools are cheap too. One on one classes run around $5/hour. Most of the schools offer to arrange home stays with local families at very good rates.

Antigua is famous for its language schools, and famous for the thousands of young students who flock to them for three reasons: to have fun, to have fun, and to learn Spanish. Mom and Dad pay for all this of course. Most of the schools feature optional group activities in the afternoons:

STUDYING SPANISH

salsa dancing classes and trips to local touristic sites and handicraft centers are typical.

Actually, I find my fellow students to be of all ages, from all over the world. It seems there are usually more European students than North Americans.

Most schools offer "full-immersion" learning experiences as well as extensive formal one-on-one classroom study to students from all over the world. The town is full of young and old students from North America, Europe, Israel and Asia, attracted by the inexpensive week- and two-week-long courses. Most of the students, but certainly not all, are young university types. Local wags realize the many students come to their schools for three reasons: to have fun, to have fun, and to learn Spanish. The town is appropriately full of great bars and dance spots.

I have heard students complaining that they find themselves spending far more time speaking English during their time in Guatemala than they would like, because Antigua has so many tourists and stu-

dents hanging around in the same bars they like to hang around in. If you spend your time with other students and travelers you meet, this may well be true for you too. Most schools organize extracurricular activities for their students, such as salsa dancing, cooking or other lessons and visits to nearby sites of interest.

Christian Spanish Academy
The largest and best-known school in Antigua is the quite professional Christian Spanish Academy. Teachers and employees all wear uniforms. Originally established to teach Spanish to foreign missionaries, the school has changed into a well-run for-profit educational institute. Their special focus programs include

business, flight attendant, ecology, civilization & culture, children and veterinary language studies. They receive high ratings on websites like www.guatemala365.com that rate language schools.

Info: 6a Avenida Norte #15. www.learncsa.com; Tel. 502-7832-3922.

Academia de Español Antigüeña

The two weeks I spent studying here were well worth the time and small cost. I had a one-on-one, four-our session every morning. On some days, my teacher went around town with me to museums, the craft market, etc. conversing with me and teaching as we walked. I met a bunch of other students and participated in some "extra-curricular activities." My Spanish was midlevel and still is, but I vastly improved my comprehension and use of irregular verbs.

The school runs 20 morning and 20 afternoon, four-hour, one-on-one sessions with 20 teachers and 20 students. Each teacher and student have their own private work area with a blackboard, desk and two chairs. The school has developed its own printed study materials and the teachers are all university trained. For students not in classes, there are a variety of organized activities offered such as salsa dance classes, tours of local cathedrals and churches, visits to coffee local farms and such.

The school offers courses developed especially for students interested in focusing on medical, legal, engineering and general business language skills.

The owner, Julio, is a blast and keeps a careful eye on everything. He runs a tight ship but the atmosphere is one of fun. The staff and teachers seem to be quite happy with their work and work environment. Academia Antigüeña is rated number one on www.guatemala365.com, which is why I selected it. I have visited and reviewed several schools, but I went back to the same school for another week a few months later because I liked it so much the first time.

Info: 1a. Calle Poniente #10, Tel. 502-7832-7241, www.spanishacademyantiguena.com.

BEST SPORTS & RECREATION

Hiking, Parks & Eco Walks
Antigua Tours
by Elizabeth Bell

Noted historian Elizabeth Bell has created a nice business leading and arranging tours of Antigua and the surrounding attractions. Her three-hour cultural tours take in all the main sights of Antigua from museums to churches. Both Ms. Bell herself and assistants lead tours. **Hillary Clinton** has been on the tour. You can use her travel services for more than just walking tours around town. She arranges one of the best tours to **Volcán Pacaya** (*see photo at right*) and runs shuttle services to most of the popular touristic destinations in the country. Prices are a little higher than even the big name competing shuttle companies, but she is known for running top-quality vehicles with friendly, English-speaking guides and drivers. Her web site is well done, with plenty of detailed information about her tours and transportation services.

Info: 3a Calle Oriente #22, (next door to Hotel Casa Santo Domingo) and 5a Avenida Norte #6 (inside Café el Por-

tal). www.antiguatours.net; Tel. 502-7832-5821, 502-7832-2046.

Volcano Climbing Scene

Volcano climbs happen every day and leave from Panajachel, Antigua and Guatemala City. They are easy to arrange for half day, full day or even overnight hikes. Dress warm; it's cold on top. Some of the more spectacular climbs include the ever-spouting **Pacaya**. Some lava heads go so far as to spend the night on top of the volcano to better enjoy the sunrise. It gets *very* cold up there. Other volca-

SPORTS & RECREATION

noes may be quite a climb but yield little more than a meager view from a heavily-wooded peak. Three companies stand out and can arrange for hikes leaving from most of the major towns.

Kukulkan Travel & Tours in Panajachel can arrange for visits to Volcán San Pedro, Toliman, Atitlán, Tajumulco and Pacaya from most major cities.

Info: Tel. 502-7820-8031.

Elizabeth Bell, with offices in Antigua, arranges one of the best tours to Volcán Pacaya from most major cities.

Info: 3a Calle Oriente #22, (next door to Hotel Casa Santo Domingo) and 5a Avenida

Norte #6 (inside Café el Portal). www.antiguatours.net; Tel. 502-7832-5821, 502-7832-2046.

OX Outdoor Excursions specializes in overnight trips to volcanoes Acatenango, Pacaya, Fuego and Santiaguito.

Info: Tel: 502-5801-4301; 1st. Ave. South # 4b- 1A. Ave. Sur # 4b.

Valhalla Macadamia Nut Farm
About 15 minutes outside town, Valhalla is a working macadamia nut farm with facilities for showing tourists around. The simple English- and Spanish-language tour explains the history of nut production in general and of the farm itself. A small shop sells nuts, nut butter and other macadamia products including facial creams. Samples and facial creaming sessions are offered. It is a pleasant and shady place, but of only mild interest overall, unless you happen to be a macadamia nut nut.

Info: Tel. 502-7831-5799.

5. LAKE ATITLÁN

HIGHLIGHTS

▲ Kayaking – an almost mystical experience

▲ Circus Bar – great live music

▲ Lakeside Villages – picturesque villages around the lake

COORDINATES

Three huge volcanic cones loom over the stunningly beautiful **Lake Atitlán**. Tourist and Mayan town **Panajachel** is the easiest of the lakeside villages to get to and has the most hotels and restaurants in the area. The lake is about a three hour drive from Guatemala City.

INTRO

The stunning Lake Atitlán, surrounded by classic volcanic cones, rivals any lake or other landscape you can think of in the world for magnificence. I compare it to the Grand Canyon or Bora-Bora. For me, Lake Atitlán is one of the most beautiful places in the world. Colorful Mayan people populate the lakeside villages. Festering bohemian communities add appealing flavor.

SIGHTS

LAKE ATITLÁN IN A DAY

Panajachel, Santiago de Atitlán and **San Pedro** are the main towns around the stunningly beautiful Lake Atitlán. Panajachel is the easiest of the towns to get to, and is a good base for exploring the numerous small villages around the lake. Pana also has great shopping, a good selection of hotels, interesting restaurants (some with great views of the lake) and several happening nightspots. In one day, you can visit several lakeside villages by launch, and still have time to shop and eat dinner in Panajachel.

Morning
Touristy **Panajachel** has great shopping, eating, and drink-ing. It's a nice little town in a stunning location. But, with only one day to explore the lake, if you get hung up in Pana for long, you won't have time to see very much else. Besides, as you walk down **Calle Santander** (the main tourist street in town) on your way to the docks, you'll see most of what the town has to offer. Stop and check out the fabrics, carvings and other tourist goodies on sale from the stalls that line the street.

Panajachel has a very **good selection of typical Guatemalan fabrics and handicrafts**. The shops and stalls in Panajachel will have most of the things you are likely to want to buy as you travel

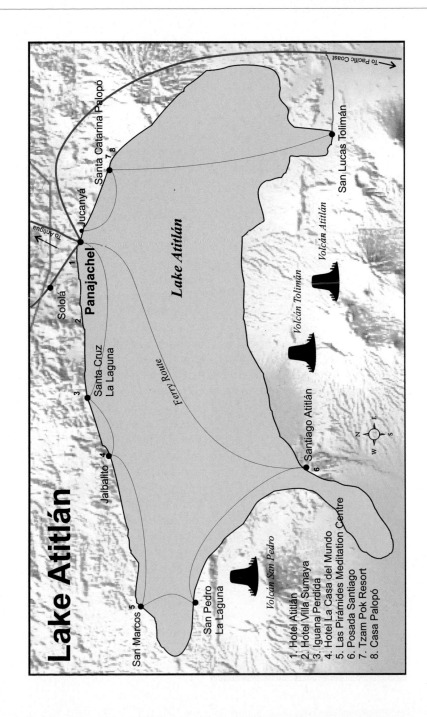

Lake Atitlán

1. Hotel Atitlán
2. Hotel Villa Sumaya
3. Iguana Perdida
4. Hotel La Casa del Mundo
5. Las Pirámides Meditation Centre
6. Posada Santiago
7. Tzam Pok Resort
8. Casa Palopó

SIGHTS

around the lake. Since Pana is a market center for Lake Atitlán artisans, the selection will usually be bigger and the prices, possibly, lower. Bargain, bargain, bargain. At the dock, try to avoid the touts and line up a trip on a *lancha* across the lake to **San Pedro**.

There are two docks in San Pedro. One is where boats from Pana and villages on that side of the lake dock, and the other is where boats for Santiago and San Lucas dock. There are two roads up into the town from the two docks. Both are a bit steep, but trudge on up to the church and market, where the two more or

less meet, and then skip on downhill to the other dock. By the Santiago dock, grab a coffee at **La Piscina San Pedro**. It's an open air bar with reasonable food, a pool and a wonderful lake view. Have a cold beer, then wander around town. Take another *lancha colectivo* to **Hotel La Casa del Mundo** just past Jaibalito where you can have a lovely lunch overlooking the lake. Let the view hypnotize you.

Afternoon

You can swim from the dock and **rent kayaks** from Casa del Mundo if you feel you have time to hang around for a couple of hours. When you get tired, flag down another *lancha* and head back to Panajachel. Do any last-minute shopping on Calle Santander and settle down at a secluded table at **Sunset Café** for sunset happy hour and some live music. The view is simply awesome. Don't eat here. There are much better choices nearby.

Evening

There are several good places to eat in Pana and one great one. The great one, **Chez Alex**, is a straight-ahead, proper Ital-

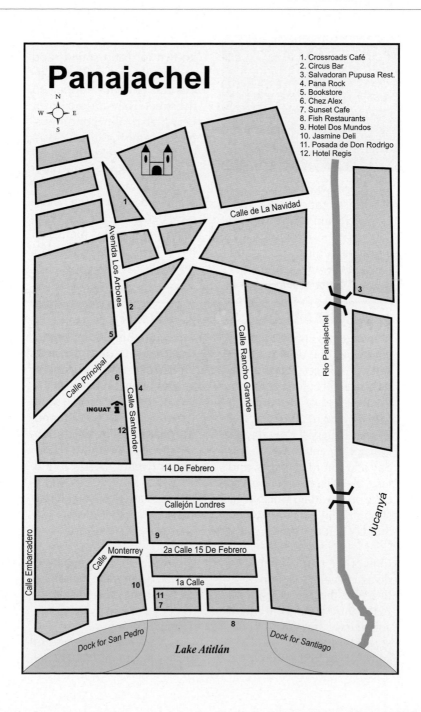

Panajachel

1. Crossroads Café
2. Circus Bar
3. Salvadoran Pupusa Rest.
4. Pana Rock
5. Bookstore
6. Chez Alex
7. Sunset Cafe
8. Fish Restaurants
9. Hotel Dos Mundos
10. Jasmine Deli
11. Posada de Don Rodrigo
12. Hotel Regis

SIGHTS

ALTERNATE PLAN
Take a *lancha* in the morning from Panajachel to laid back **Santiago** for the day. You can visit other nearby villages by *lancha* during the day on your way back.

ian place with linen table-cloths, a good wine list, carpaccio and fresh seafood.

If you are a music lover and have the evening free after dinner, **Pana Rock** is well known for Latin sounds and regular old rock and roll. **Circus Bar** is a little further up the street. They are known for very high quality performers, mostly in the traditional Spanish flamenco style. Things get going about 8pm. They often have several different performances each evening. Monday nights are usually "anything can happen" nights. If I am in town, I'll be there. The pizzas are good too.

A WEEKEND IN LAKE ATITLÁN

A weekend is enough time to check out one or two of the smaller villages around the lake and still enjoy the touristic pleasures of the festering tourist town, **Panajachel** (Pana). I suggest you stay in Panajachel and party on Friday and Saturday nights, and visit the villages around the Lake on Saturday. Finish your shopping in Panajachel on Sunday before leaving.

One of the hardest things to do as a travel writer is to try to describe the most beautiful places in the world. It might sound easy, but how do I describe something as awesomely beautiful as the Grand Canyon or Bora-Bora without using the same old tired words I use to describe the beautiful garden at my home? You just can't do it. How do you separate the ordinarily astoundingly beautiful beach, mountain or vista from the five or ten or twenty *most* astoundingly beautiful places on the entire planet? I quickly exhaust Microsoft Word's thesaurus trying to do so.

Simply put, for me, Lake Atitlán is one of the most beautiful places I have visited.

Friday Evening
There are several wonderful places to stay in Panajachel.

Just outside town, the most beautiful lodging in the area is, without a doubt, the **Hotel Atitlán**. They have one of the best restaurants on the lake and are a short tuk-tuk ride into town.

If you have time after arriving and checking in, take a tuk-tuk into town and stroll up and down **Calle Santander** marveling at the beautiful fabrics and elaborate carved masks for sale in the hundreds of tourist stalls. There are several small internet cafés good for a quick coffee and email check.

Around sunset, it's always a good idea to head to the bottom of the street and the **Sunset Café**. They have a happy hour and live music every evening at the expected time. The food here is not particularly good and the service is glacial, but the views are stupendous and you can usually get a fairly secluded table stuck away in the bushes. I like the place but don't eat anything other than, perhaps, nachos. The beer is cold.

Some people will be quite happy to see only the part of Panajachel seen as you walk from where the bus drops you off to the boat dock. There's actually not much more to see, so don't feel guilty if you fall into that category. It's a tourist town—but a nice one. Grab a *lancha* for San Pedro and chill.

Saturday
In the morning, visit San Pedro, on the other side of the lake below **Volcán San Pedro**. You can go into Pana and get on a *colectivo* or, for substan-

SMOKE?

Due to its location halfway between the drug sources in South America and the consumers in the US, Guatemala has a growing drug problem. Secret jungle airstrips abound in the Petén region. Some locals indulge and some visiting tourists look for a doper-friendly lifestyle. *Mota*, as the cheap marijuana is known locally, is certainly available, as is cheap cocaine. Old hippies back in the hills around Lake Atitlán grow *mangito*, the good stuff, using Canadian seeds. The quality competes with the best from anywhere in the world. Our advice: stay as far away from this scene as possible.

SIGHTS

SIGHTS

tially more money, let the hotel arrange for a personal *lancha* to take you there. San Pedro is nice for a long visit but even if you can only spend an hour or two it's worth it. At least walk up the steep street from the dock and marvel at the church at the top of the hill and visit the art galleries on the way. There is a small fruit/vegetable/everything market almost next door. Another steep street runs downhill to the other dock—the town has two. *Lanchas* to the west end of the lake usually go to one dock. On the other side of town, boats for the east side of the lake do their thing. I kind of like having a beer at one of the restaurant/bars by either dock. I like to hang at **La Piscina San Pedro** near the Santiago dock.

Goof off in San Pedro for a while and then take a *colectivo* to the **Santa Cruz** and head for the excellent **Iguana Perdida**. This is quite a popular hangout spot for travelers young and old. The Iguana is a relatively inexpensive restaurant/bar/hotel, and also arranges scuba diving and the usual lake activities. They have a lot to offer. It is a good, casual place to meet other travelers. The views of the lake from the terrace are spectacular. Stay there for lunch, swim, lie about and then flag down a colectivo heading for Pana and stop off in **Jaibalito**.

Just outside Jaibalito is the wonderful lakeside **Hotel La Casa del Mundo**. The hotel spills down the hillside to the lake, and has dozens of private little hangout spots tucked away in the gardens, with hypnotizing views of the lake. The restaurant has the usual lake and local Guate/Mex stuff, but it's very nicely done. You can visit and swim, rent kayaks and otherwise enjoy the lake in a pleasant atmosphere. The water seems especially clean here.

After enjoying lunch and swimming or kayaking, grab

a passing lancha and head to Pax Anax (pronounced *posh anosh*), a very small lakeside village that is home to some exquisite lakeside homes and the wonderful **Hotel Villa Sumaya** and the luxurious **Laguna Lodge**. There is a path along the shoreline that is wonderful for a stroll. I'm not sure how far you can go on this path along the lake. I usually poop out about this time of day and, after a mile or so, I find a convenient dock and flag down a *lancha* heading to Pana.

After dinner, you could simply stroll back to your room and collapse into bed, or go back into town for a little nightlife, live music and adult beverages. **Pana Rock** on Calle Santander is guaranteed to pop your eardrums with both Latin music and rock and roll. **Circus Bar** (*see photo above right*), a little further up the street, usually has live flamenco or classic Latin sounds. It's my favorite. Monday night is basically "anything can happen night," with a variety of local musicians dropping in until late, late. A couple of the open air restaurants in town have guitarists and/or singers on some nights. I like to wan-

der around listening for music and drop in for a beer or two wherever there are sounds that attract me.

Sunday

Rent a kayak on the beach for an almost psychedelic view of the lake. Few activities are as relaxing and as awe-inspiring as drifting quietly a few hundred feet offshore. The reflections of the surrounding volcanoes on the water create a magical scene. I love to do this in the early morning when the winds are usually non-existent. You can feel the powerful cosmic energy of the energetic matrix as you drift along.

Go back to the hotel and shower off. Last minute shopping is easy in Pana. The half-mile long **Calle Santander** is lined with shops selling colorful fabrics, wild masks and carvings. Walk a little and shop. Take a shuttle to your

SIGHTS

next destination. Most of the shuttles stop running at 4pm so plan carefully so you don't end up stranded on the wrong side of the lake for the night.

A WEEK IN & AROUND LAKE ATITLÁN

There is a lot to do around the lake. **Panajachel** (Pana), a good base for exploring the many unique waterfront villages, has dozens of agencies aimed at helping tourists decide how to spend their days. Boat trips to small lakeside villages, coffee farm tours, visits to Mayan fabric production cooperatives, scuba diving (yes, you can!), fishing for black bass, paragliding, eco-hiking, screaming zip lines (if you must), boat tours, yoga retreats, spiritual healing sessions, full moon drumming parties, kayaking and *so much more* are all on offer. That should be enough. But you can also go to Spanish school, volunteer to help local communities, go birding or even learn traditional Mayan healing techniques. Be sure to find out what your birth sign is in the Mayan calendar.

Spend the first night in Panajachel to get oriented and secure any tourist supplies you might need. One by one, visit

some of the beautiful lakeside villages, staying in interesting hotels as you go. After a night in Pana, take a *lancha* in the morning to Santiago for a few nights. You can visit other nearby villages by *lancha* during the day. Then, take a *lancha* to **Villa Sumaya** in Jaibalito for a little yoga and Tai Chi. Spend your last couple of days high above the lake at **Tzam Pok** in Santa Catarina Palopó, where you can bake yourself in their wood-fired sauna and stare at the volcanoes over the rim of their infinity pool.

For me, Lake Atitlán is one of the most beautiful places in the world. Need I say more? I'm a writer; of course I'm going to say more.

When I am around Lake Atitlán, I feel a steady, peaceful power of some kind filling the environment around me. I have hung around in tropical beach towns where the booming sound of the huge surf dominated the entire environment, acting as a hypnotic narcotic and making it impossible for me to clear my head and leave for the next town. The **soporific beauty and spiritual aura** of Lake Atitlán are as powerful a narcotic as was the sound of that booming surf. Sun, clouds and psychic vortices constantly change the personality of the lake surface, the volcanoes and the sky. What a scene!

Panajachel, San Pedro and the other small villages around the lake benefit from a **festering bohemian community**. Unusual thinkers, beats like **Aldous Huxley**, aging hippies, and "real" travelers have been coming to the area for decades, and many have never left. The communities around the lake, particularly **Jucanyá**, just across the river from Panajachel, attract not only Guatemalan artists, artisans, musicians and poets, but interesting international people of the same ilk.

Each village around the lake has its own style of fabrics and handicrafts. **San Jorge and Santa Palopó**, both near Panajachel, are known for their woven reed mats. San Lucas Toliman produces hand-carved furniture. **San Pedro La Laguna** produces hand-woven rugs. San Marcos is known for rope and cordage in general.

SIGHTS

Calle Santander, the main road up from the docks in Panajachel, is lined with seemingly **hundreds of shops and stalls** selling traditional and tourist-oriented items from all over Guatemala. The selection is awesome. Still, it is worthwhile to travel around the lake, visiting the smaller towns and villages to see for yourself what is produced locally. Panajachel, San Pedro and Santiago all have shops selling things of interest to visitors but, in the smaller villages, there are few shops that you will find to be of much touristic interest.

Panajachel
Pana is the most touristed village on the lake and has plenty of lodgings in all price categories, many restaurants (some very good), happening

nightspots and some of the best shopping in Guatemala. It's a good place to start your visit to the lake or to use as a base for exploring the lake villages on day trips. It is very popular with young, international travelers and is a good place to make new friendships among the cool people who flock there.

Pana and nearby Jucanyá are home to Guatemala's **festering musical and artistic colony**, so there are interesting happenings in the bars and nightspots around town as well as a plethora of artists and artisans selling oil paintings, jewelry, masks and a huge selection of the colorful fabrics Guatemala is so famous for.

There are several live music venues with Latin, rock and traditional Mayan performances. Circus Bar, Pana Rock, and Sunset Café almost always have good-quality performers.

Santa Catarina Palopó
Santa Catarina Palopó, only a couple of miles from Pana, has a very distinctive weaving style. You can easily tell which Mayan women are

from that area by their bright blue *huipiles,* skirts and head cloths. Several shops along the main street sell these. You can also find them in the stalls in Pana. **Casa Palopó** and **Tzam Pok**, located just outside the village, are two of the lake's most interesting and luxurious lodgings. I love them both.

San Lucas Tolimán
At the east end of the lake, San Lucas is lower in altitude than the other lake towns and enjoys some of the warmth of the Pacific lowlands that flows up the valley below the village. It is accessible by boat or difficult road. Perhaps it's not as pretty a village as most others around the lake, but you can see palm trees and walk along the shore for a different angle for photos of the imposing volcanoes surrounding the lake.

Santiago Atitlán
Santiago is a largish, bustling town of no particular beauty. The street up from the dock is lined with tourist stalls and boasts some of the most aggressive kids hustling beads and cloth, and hoping to lead you to hotels or to visit the disquieting **Maximón**. Just

ALTERNATE PLAN
Skip all this running around and changing hotels. Check into the upscale bohemian **Tzam Pok** and let them arrange *lanchas* and taxis for you. Much easier, very tranquil, and you can marinate in their wood-fired sauna every morning.

SIGHTS

outside town is the wonderful **Posada de Santiago**, one of my favorite places to stay in Guatemala.

Santiago is probably most famous for the horrible massacre that occurred there during the recent war. Local residents rose successfully against the army that was stationed in their peaceful town, after several soldiers raped a local shopkeeper's daughter. To this day, on orders of the President, the military keeps strictly away from Santiago. Read Bonny Dilger's *Blood in the Cornfields* for a frightening account of the massacre and life in those times. By the way, she owns and used to run the Posada de Santiago.

Santiago is also famous as the center of the cult of **Maximón** (pronounced mashimón). Maximón is actually a small

WHAT IS ECOTOURISM, ANYWAY?

Ecotourism is a term that you'll hear kicked around quite a bit on your travels in Guatemala. Of course, most visitors to the area are here to enjoy the natural wonders, but does that make us all ecotourists? Does spending a couple of hours strolling through the forest with a herd of other tourists make you an ecotourist? Or must you spend a week helping the students with their research at some remote biological station to earn the title?

In fact, ecotourism is a state of mind, **an ideal of sustainable, minimally invasive tourism** that both visitors and those in the tourism industry should strive for (alas, both groups often fall far short of the ideal). Ecotourists leave no litter, don't feed or interfere with the animals, and consume nothing but products that are harvested in a sustainable manner. A true ecolodge recycles and conserves, releases no waste into the environment, strives to use renewable energy, and generally tries to have as little impact on the natural habitat as possible.

Ecotourism is also about preserving a very important species called local workers. One of the central concepts of ecotourism is the idea that local people can make a better living by helping tourists enjoy the rain forest than they could by chopping it down. Good ecotourists patronize local businesses, and buy local products whenever possible.

The **International Ecotourism Society** defines ecotourism as "responsible travel to natural areas that conserves the environment and improves the well-being of local people." Their web site at **www.ecotourism.org** includes lists of environmentally friendly lodges and tour operators.

dummy fixed up to smoke cigars and drink booze. He is addicted to all sorts of bad behavior. The keepers of his shrine expect visitors to placate their demons by providing him (the dummy) with beer, whiskey, rum, cigarettes, cigars and other fun things. If you decide to make such a donation, you get to whisper your needs to the spirit of Maximón and, perhaps, receive a message or advice. It is *possible* that his acolytes consume the bulk of these offerings themselves. It's good fun. You *have* to visit!

Believe it or not, **bass fishing** is spectacular on the lake. This is the same bass that rednecks (and myself) in the Southern US spend thousands of dollars chasing around in high-powered bass boats. They grow to over 20 pounds in the approximately 1,500-foot depths of the lake. Martin Chif, in Santiago, owns a local gas

station and provides boat and all the tackle you need to haul in a lunker. Take a camera. Your buddies back in Arkansas will not believe you. The best time is late afternoon, and he takes two people out for about $75. Quite a bargain.

Santiago is filthy with history and interesting archeological sites. Much Mayan culture remains, and ruins of colonial architecture are everywhere. The local inhabitants, mostly **Tz'utujil Mayans**, have preserved much of their culture and have created an interesting fusion of the imposed European customs and their own ancient traditions.

For colorful and **educational walking tours** through the town of Santiago, **Dolores Ratzán** speaks excellent English and has expert knowledge of Tz'utujil culture and customs, particularly its folk Catholicism. She takes guests to all the churches and historical sites, and finishes her two-hour tours with a visit to a weaving workshop and, if you like, to the market and handicraft stalls to help you purchase local handicrafts and art.

SIGHTS

Amanda Chif, former Peace Corps volunteer, will take you on a tour via tuk-tuk (small, three-wheeled taxi-like conveyance) to all the sites in and around town. This is a safe and relaxing way for those of us with failing knees, etc. to get to the local sites.

San Pedro La Laguna
San Pedro caters to a hip young crowd of international travelers. It is known for having perhaps the cheapest Spanish language schools in the country, and for being a little down-at-the-heels. It is well loved by *mochileros* (backpackers) for its nightlife. Happening bars/hangout spots include the famous **Freedom Bar**, which has live music with **big** speakers, the **Flying Dog Reggae Bar** and the **Buddha Bar**. There are several other places to absorb good nighttime vibrations. You can also rent kayaks, horses and scooters for trips to the nearby volcano or to visit other, nearby villages. This is a hippie town, and many of the small local shops offer a wide selection of rolling papers.

Nick's Place is a good spot to enjoy a drink or meal while waiting for a ferry. The views are great, the sounds are nice and the drinks are cold. Fish is usually the local *mojara*. Touts at the dock are fairly laid back and may actually be useful for finding and engaging guides for the volcano climb or other groovy activities.

San Marcos La Laguna
Pleasant and shady San Marcos presents the best of Lake Atitlán's **new age vortex exploration,** particularly well represented by the fascinating **Las Pirámides Meditation Centre**.

Surrounded by lush vegetation and right on the shore of the lake, the centre has two meditation temples, pyramid-shaped cabins, a library, medicinal herb garden, communal kitchen, sauna, and a vegetarian restaurant. This is a "study centre" rather than a hotel. Guests participate in daily meditation and yoga sessions. The medicinal plant sauna is a great way to start the day. Courses include meditation techniques, **introductions to astral travel**, vibrations or dimensions, astrology, and numerology sessions. **Fasting** and **periods of** complete **silence** round out the month-long **moon course**. One must complete the moon course before moving on to the **sun course**.

There are several good restaurants/bars here. **Blind Lemon's** restaurant/bar is cool, has regular blues nights, great food and wi-fi. **Il Giardino** is an Italian restaurant offering daily specials like lasagna, Greek salad, etc. and **Paco Real** is a quiet hotel/restaurant with palapa-roofed bungalows. It seems a little crowded in their small garden area and is not fancy but it's plenty charming. Mexican food is on offer.

El Jaibalito

West of Pana a bit, accessible only by boat or foot path, is the village of El Jaibalito. You can easily flag down passing *lanchas* for rides to Pana or San Pedro. There are nice walks along the shore on either side of town but the main point of interest is the nice **Hotel La Casa del Mundo** (*see photo at right*). It is really too far from Pana for evening expeditions but would be good for lunch trips. They have a wood fire-heated hot tub and great swimming areas.

Santa Cruz La Laguna

There is a wonderful walk along the lake between Santa Cruz and **Pax Anax** (pawsh aw nosh). A path runs along the edge of the lake, passing luxurious homes and quaint hotels with fabulous views of the lake. You can walk out onto any dock and flag down a passing *lancha* when you've had enough walking.

The **Iguana Perdida** is a large, decent backpacker hotel restaurant/bar/tourism center that stares you in the face as soon as you get off the boat. They can arrange for **diving**, **kayak rentals** and other activities. They have a nice restaurant where you can stare at the volcanoes and sip your drink.

Nearby, **Hotel Villa Sumaya** has good lounging areas with comfortable chairs and hammocks. Stop by their gift shop as you walk along the lakeside.

BEST SLEEPS & EATS

Panajachel offers a wide variety of lodging, with seemingly dozens of dorm-like hostels, a few mid-priced options and one high-end lodging choice. The villages around the lake each seem to have a couple of backpacker hotels and one or two better places. **Casa Palopó** in Santa Catarina, **Dos Mundos** and **Laguna Lodge** in Jaibalito and **Hotel Atitlán** outside Pana are the stars of the show.

Like most tourist towns, Panajachel is packed with small restaurants offering pizza, burgers, pasta and Mexicanish food to the passing tourist hordes. Around the lake there are four or five outstanding places to eat. Most of the other places serve okay food but, after a while, they all seem pretty much the same. There are a few gringo-run eateries that have slightly different offerings.

PANAJACHEL
There are dozens of small hotels in and around the town, offering everything from serious luxury to backpacker rooms. You can spend several hundred dollars a night or less than $5.

Hotel Regis $$
Most of the hotel seems newish, with well-appointed rooms, but some of the rooms are a little older and need a little attention from maintenance staff. The hotel is conveniently located right in the middle of town next to the school. Things can get noisy in the afternoons when the kids are in the schoolyard doing rowdy school kid things. Hot springs bubble up right on the hotel property into two very nice hot tubs. This is a great place for a late

night soak with someone special. With a little notice, they will fire up the sauna for you. I am not fond of the restaurant. The breakfasts are skimpy and overpriced, considering there are at least a dozen better places to eat within a 2-minute walk. The

BEST OF THE BEST IN ATITLÁN

Hotel Atitlán $$$

Perhaps the most beautiful hotel in the country, the Atitlán oozes charm, and is choked with antiques and wonderful examples of Guatemalan art and fabrics. The 65 rooms and suites are arranged in several wings of a Spanish colonial-style building set in an amazing, immaculately-maintained botanical garden with exotic plants from all over Guatemala. The setting is right on the lake, just a little way outside Panajachel. All rooms have private balconies and spectacular views of the lake. You can simply turn your head on your pillow and enjoy the sight of the brilliant lake and surrounding volcanoes.

The rooms are large, well furnished and stylish, with nice showers. There is no AC, but the high altitude means you will probably need another blanket instead of AC. The gift shop is particularly well stocked with local crafts and fabrics. The restaurant is excellent and the two bars quite comfortable. Their web site, although beautiful and sporting up to the minute graphics and technical wizardry, is low on actual information, like phone numbers. I had a fairly hard time contacting and conversing with them. Their wi-fi works reasonably well in the rooms closest to the lobby.

This is one of the most beautiful hotels I have visited in Guatemala. *Info: Panajachel. www.hotelatitlan.com; Tel. 502-2360-8405, 502-2360-8415.*

last time I stayed they had a breakfast buffet which was fine but too expensive. *Info: Panajachel. Tel. 502-7762-1149, 502-7762-2120, www.hotelregisatitlan.com.*

Posada de Don Rodrigo $$$

This is by far the nicest hotel choice in town. The rooms are comfortable, large and decorated in high Mayan style with sculptures, masks on the walls and brightly-colored local fabrics covering everything they can figure out how to cover. The pool is large and has a water slide for the kids. Large tour buses disgorge tourist hordes but somehow the place never seems to be overcrowded. The staff are quite friendly.

The restaurant is a little sterile but serves good food with extremely good service. Even the busboy and coffee lady remember your name and use it every time they come to the table. The food is the usual chicken, steaks, Mexican stuff and local fish but is nicely done. Prices are significantly higher than in the restaurants on Calle Santander but the food is of slightly higher quality. They serve great coffee and have wonderful views of the lake. I suggest sitting outside on the patio where things aren't quite so loud and the views are even better. I love to have breakfast here. *Info: Final Calle Santander, Panajachel. www.posadadedonrodrigo.com; Tel. 502-7762-2326.*

Dos Mundos $$

Conveniently located in its own quiet courtyard near the middle of Calle Santander, Dos Mundos offers a medium-priced, comfortable lodging option. Some rooms are in a conventional two-story hotel building, but the nicest ones are grouped around a nice pool and garden area. This is a good choice if you have kids—the pool is shallow and there is plenty of room for them to

SLEEPS & EATS

run around. Rooms are peaceful with cable TV, hot water and comfortable, if a little worn, bedding. Service is friendly. The included breakfast, served at their poolside restaurant,

is just adequate. They have good parking near the rooms. *Info: Calle Santender #4-72, Panajachel. www.hoteldosmundos.com; Tel. 502-7762-2078.*

DINING OUT IN PANA

Pana is loaded with restaurants, street stalls and bars. Most of them serve pretty much the same selection of chicken, beef, pasta, tilapia, shrimp and Mexicanish food. There are a couple of standouts though.

The **"fish restaurants"** refers to a group of run-down-looking wooden deck-like structures packed with plastic chairs and tables at the edge of the lake—with spectacular views, of course. Follow your way east along the waterfront towards the river and you will encounter dozens of these fish restaurants. Touts lurk in front of each waving menus. They are almost all the same. In fact, you may notice that when you place your order, the waiter runs outside and downstairs or down the street to another restaurant, which is where your food is actually cooked. No problem. It seems many of the restaurants are actually sharing the same kitchen. I find the food to be poor and the prices high whenever I have visited, but the views are some of the finest in the world and the beer is always cold. All seem to be infested with street urchins selling grubby jewelry items but the views are tremendous.

Best of the Best – Hotel Atitlán $$$
A great place for breakfast, the restaurant at the Hotel Atitlán has very good food and great atmosphere. They have an extensive

wine list with selections mainly from Chile, Argentina and Spain. Waitstaff are dressed in elaborate, really over-the-top outfits based on traditional Mayan attire. Their chicken soup is probably the best I have ever had.

The dining room has high ceilings with dark beams and is loaded with antiques. Table settings include colorful local weavings in the form of table runners, tablecloths, placemats and napkins. The food is well prepared and includes many local specialties as well as not-so-local entrees like shrimp cocktail, salmon and Chilean sea bass. Even if you are not a regular tea drinker, you should set aside a half hour to enjoy one of their exotic tea infusions in the tranquil bar just off the restaurant. They have dozens of types of loose tea stored in sealed jars. This is not a tea bag thing. They actually brew the tea in small teapots. Imagine that! *Info: Panajachel. www.hotelatitlan.com; Tel. 502-2360-8405.*

Circus Bar $$

This is a nice place to stop for a pizza in the evening; there is almost always live music. It can get crowded and rowdy with locals and gringos sucking down beer from quart bottles. The décor features circus posters and other circus paraphernalia. The pizza is supposed to be "the best in town." I don't know about that particular claim, but the pizza is excellent with lots of cheese. Most pizza lovers will be well pleased. *See photo on page 85. Info: Panajachel, located just past the end of Calle Santander. Open 12-12.*

El Bistro $$

Reasonably good Italian fare with local influences. Paul Newman or somebody was rumored to have used the place as his personal dining room while staying in the area. I eat here from time to time and usually get the *lomito al limón*. Nice. *Info: Panajachel, Calle Santander near the bottom.*

Restaurante Jebel $$
Right across the street from Hotel Regis on the second floor. Grab a table with a view of the always interesting street traffic. The food is regular old fish, burgers and chicken. I like their *camarones al ajillo* (shrimp with garlic). *Info: Panajachel, Calle Santander.*

Chez Alex $$$$
If you are tired of pizza, burgers, burritos and beans and want a proper European-style meal with all the trimmings, Chez Alex is your next stop. When you walk in, white linen table cloths and napkins, waiters wearing fancy, European-style waiter outfits and the wonderful smell of garlic put you in the mood for fantastic pasta, carpaccio and steaks. The wonderful meals are not cheap— this is by far the nicest restaurant in town and you have to pay for that. Service is spot-on and the food consistently delicious. Their wine list is small but good. It is also pricey. Nice wines are expensively imported in Guatemala so, in restaurants, you don't see many bottles under $20—most run over $40. I come here at least once a week when I am in the area. I always leave with a full belly, a warm buzz and a smile on my face. I like Chez Alex. *Info: Panajachel, Calle Santander. Tel. 502-7762-0172.*

Sunset Café $$
Everyone who comes to Panajachel wants to find a nice place to eat, drink and relax with a fantastic view of the lake and surrounding volcanoes. This is the spot. The restaurant/bar is perched on a hill at the bottom of Calle Santander with an almost unbeatable view. The palapa-covered area is comfortable with plenty of sort-of-private tables in between plants. The view is mesmerizing, which helps since the food is only in the okay category. The usual fish, chicken and pork meals are on offer, with a broad selection of Mexican-style dishes familiar to US palates like fajitas, quesadillas and enchiladas. They do have one of the better burgers in town. *Info*: Panajachel, Calle Santander near the bottom.

Jasmine Deli $$
The Deli is a solid, small restaurant at the bottom of Calle Santander. Local expats use it as a hangout and meeting place.

The tables are mostly shade covered, with a couple in a garden near the back. The food is better than at most of the small eating joints along Santander, with brewed coffee, the usual sandwiches and bagels, English muffins, pita bread with humus and some interesting deserts. I like the banana pancakes in the morning and a chicken sandwich on an English muffin for lunch. It's a very relaxing place but I find the wait staff to be indifferent. *Info: Panajachel, Calle Santander near the bottom.*

Guajimbo's Parrillada $$

If you are in the mood for roasted meat, meat and more meat, this is a good choice. The steaks are a little tougher than what you are probably used to in North America but are quite flavorful. I like the pork chops and smoked sausage. They usually have quite good live music in the evenings, as the owner is a guitarist and live music enthusiast himself. Skip it if you're looking for fine dining but it is a great spot to eat meat, drink beer, listen to excellent live music and watch the crowd on Calle Santander. *Info: Calle Santander.*

Pupuseria Bar Cheros $

At the top of Calle Principal, almost across the street from the Circus Bar, there is a little scruffy-looking, concrete block restaurant with an arched doorway serving wonderful pupusas. These Salvadoran specialties are kind of like corn pancakes stuffed with sausage, cheese, garlic, chicharrones and other delights. The pupusas are prepared to order so it takes about 15 minutes before they arrive at your table smoking hot. Cover them with the included hot pickled vegetables and you've got a meal fit for a king. I like to get a seat at the bar so I can watch the ladies making the pupusas, grabbing a handful of corn meal, forming it around whatever fillings have been ordered and then patting them flat by hand. The place seems to stay open quite late. I like to stop by at the end of the evening after enjoying adult beverages and music with my friends. This is the real thing. ¡Muy auténtico! *Info: Panajachel across from Circus bar.*

Crossroads Café $$

If you are a coffee hound and want to sample some of the local beans, roasted and prepared properly, come by and visit with Mike and Adele Roberts. These guys run a small but wonderful coffee roasting and export company and sell superb filter or espresso coffees. They always have a selection of four or five fresh-roasted coffees from the surrounding area. Their place is a little hard to find but worth the hunt. Walk past Circus Bar, turn right, then left and then follow your nose. You can sample and then purchase coffee by the pound, roasted and ready to enjoy. When I am in town, I try to come by here every day. They keep odd hours (they don't open until 9:00am) and close early in the afternoon for a siesta. *Info: 0-27 Calle del Campanario. www.crossroadscafepana.com; Tel. 502-5292-8439.*

EL JAIBALITO
La Casa del Mundo $$
Spilling down a hillside overlooking the lake, Casa del Mundo is a wonderful place for honeymooners or anyone wanting to get
away from it all in a peaceful, hypnotically beautiful location. Most rooms are fairly private and all have astounding views. The restaurant offers good-quality dishes heavy on the Mexican side with family-style dinners. Perhaps the best thing
about the place is the wonderful swimming that can be done from their dock and other little outcroppings. Several small, two-person hangout spots have been carved into the side of the hill, offering very and private places to swim, sunbath, cuddle or whatever. I like this place a lot even though the rooms have become a little run-down. *Info: Near Jaibalito. www.lacasadelmundo.com; Tel. 502-5218-5332, 502-5204-5558.*

Villa Sumaya $$
Billed as a "guest house retreat center," this is an unpretentious

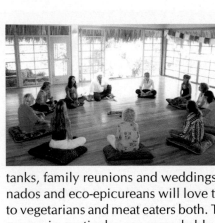

thatched roof compound with 15 luxurious rooms and two large "temples" where yoga, dance, active and sitting meditation, art groups, writing workshops, tai chi, shamanistic ceremonies, kirtan-chanting, think tanks, family reunions and weddings happen. Slow food aficionados and eco-epicureans will love the restaurant, which caters to vegetarians and meat eaters both. The hotel in general and the rooms in particular are remarkably luxurious considering the reasonable rates. They have plenty of great hammocks and comfortable lounges scattered about the grounds. Their one-week Spanish language immersion course includes lodging, all meals and one-on-one Spanish instruction for less than $100/night. What a deal! They have a solar-heated pool, hot tub and sauna.

The hotel spills down the mountainside with spectacular views of the lake and surrounding volcanoes. Rooms are simple yet quite luxurious. I like the rooms in the bungalows and Lotus House the best. *Info: Santa Cruz La Laguna. www.villasumaya.com; Tel. 502-4026-1390.*

Laguna Lodge Eco-Resort and Nature Reserve $$$$
This is one of the nicest, most luxurious lodgings on the lake. The lodge seems almost stuffed with Mayan and colonial themed artwork and antiques. Clinging to 100 acres of hillside, the rooms and restaurant seem to flow down to the lake. With high ceilings and plenty of light, the rooms are all open to the energy flowing in from the lake and volcanoes. The lodge was established with the idea of protecting, conserving and replenishing the local and global environment by utilizing responsible business practices.

Their Zotz restaurant offers "gourmet eco-cuisine" featuring fresh local legumes, free-range eggs, local cheeses and tropical fruits.

Activities include Spanish lessons, yoga study, kayaking, trips to lakeside villages and an interesting array of spa treatments.

One nice thing about Laguna Lodge is its location just a few minutes away by launch from Panajachel, Jaibalito, and some of the other laid back lakeside villages. *Info: Near Jaibalito. www.www.lagunalodgeatitlan.com; Tel. 502-7823-2529.*

SANTA CATARINA PALOPÓ

Only two miles from the bustle and fun of Panajachel, but light years away in terms of tranquility and an almost invisible spiritual power, the area around this small village is home to a couple of upscale hotels and numerous white stucco vacation homes of rich Guatemalans and gringos. The views of the villages, lake and mountains irresistibly draw your gaze. You simply cannot tear your eyes away. This is a wonderful base for exploring the villages around the lake. It is only two miles into Panajachel, so you can do all the tourist shopping and restaurant and bar hopping you like, and return easily to the matchless serenity of your hillside hideaway.

The area has dozens of elaborate homes of wealthy Guatemalans and foreigners constructed on the mountainside with tremendous views of the lake. Some can be rented by the week or month. If you have time, this is a great way to combine comfort, luxury and convenience for your extended holiday.

La Casa Colibri $$$$

This is a vacation rental. American David Yates has created a rare work of art and makes it available for rent by the week or month. His home is stunningly designed to take in the lake views, cascading down the mountainside with huge amounts of glass framing the lake and volcano panorama. The unique house is fully furnished in a fusion of American, Guatemalan and Latin chic. This is luxury and style all the way.

David is an expert in taking care of visitors providing as much or as little service as his guests desire. He can make available complete English-speaking guide services to the area, car, driver, boat trips, excursions to nearby attractions like the market at Chichicastenango, visits to lakeside villages and many out-of-the-way places only he knows about.

If you like, you can have the kitchen fully stocked and your personal chef ready to put a pizza in the wood-burning oven. You or your chef can pick fresh herbs, fruits and vegetables from the garden. Other amenities include: five master suites, deep soak tubs with lake views, infinity-edge swimming pool, sauna, games room, multiple fireplaces, and more.

David has lived in the area for years and knows how to make visitors feel at home and pampered. This is, without a doubt, the very best way to do the lake. *Info: Santa Catarina Palopó. www.lacasacolibri.com, Tel. 502-5093-6172.*

Casa Palopó $$$$
Casa Palopó is considered by many to be the finest hotel in all of Guatemala. It gets top ratings from *Conde Nast*, the *Hideaways of the Year* and other reporters on luxury lodging. With only 9 rooms, this boutique hotel offers luxury, comfort and style in one of the most picturesque settings imaginable. This is serious high-end luxury, with many guests arriving by helicopter.

Rooms are plush with Frette linens and toiletries, high-end Guatemalan and African *objets d'arte* and comfortable furnishings. Service is usually spot-on, if a little on the snooty side. Expect your fellow guests to include royalty, diplomats and privacy-seeking celebrities. Management refused (rightly so) to give me any names of famous people who have stayed here but friends reliably tell me Paris Hilton, Demi Moore and Oprah are among their celebrated clientele.

The restaurant defines some of the finest dining in Guatemala. Few people would suggest that there are any fancier places in the country, even in Guatemala City. The food is consistently won-

derful, the ambiance waaay romantic, the lake/volcano views superb. Their level of service extends to linen napkins at breakfast.

The hotel also offers two completely furnished villas—guest houses with cooks, maids and butler service. They are African-themed, decorated in high style with heated infinity pools and every conceivable luxury available. You need do little more than raise a finger, and your smallest wish becomes a reality. The villas are up the hill from the main building, and have perhaps even more stunning views than the other rooms, but you have to climb something like 180 steps to get to them.

The brilliant hotel offers overpriced tours of the lake, kayak tours, trips to the market at Chichi, one-on-one Spanish lessons and all the other standard excursions. Spirituality and wellness getaways for women of a certain age are also offered. *Info: Santa Catarina Palopó. www.casapalopo.com; Tel. 502-7762-2270, 502-5773-7777.*

Tzam Pok Resort $$$

Most visitors to Lake Atitlán expect to be happy with a couple of days in the area. Few are. Tzam Pok Resort is one of those special places in the world you just don't want to leave. There is some power in the landscape—the potential power of the looming volcanoes conflicting with the kinetic energy of the storm clouds as they tangle with the mountain tops and spill over into the lake. I like Tzam Pok because owner Lucio has combined his architectural dream of Mediteranean white stucco, dark tile, tropical

vegetation and exotic hardwoods with luxury, style and Mayan simplicity. The resort has a pool, 5 rooms and a villa, and features wonderful, wonderful food by a cook trained by owner Luciano's Italian mother. Fresh pasta, gnocci, tile, lots of white stucco, turrets, infinity pool, wood fired sauna. Rent the whole villa or adjoining terraced hillside house for a luxurious and economical way for two couples or a small group to descend into langour and luxurious laziness.

Lucio is one of those effusive Europeans with seemingly boundless energy and enthusiasm for life. Within a few minutes of basking in his smile, you realize that he is one of those people who have learned how to live. He eats, drinks, and breathes with enormous pleasure and gusto. He is a delight to talk to. Lucio and his staff make your stay special unobtrusively, putting out cushions for you to lie on next to the pool, getting up before dawn to stoke the fire in the sauna for your sweating pleasure, inquiring about your favorite foods to prepare custom-designed meals. *Info: Santa Catarina Palopó. www.atitlanresort.com; Tel. 502-7762-2680.*

Casa Palopó $$$$$

Casa Palopó is fine dining with one of the finest lake views anywhere in the world. The food is inventively prepared and presented. I find it dependably delicious. *¡Muy rico!* The ambiance rivals the quality of the food. It's located within the wonderful boutique hotel Casa Palopó, and you get to share your dinner with artists such as Botero and Ballesteros. The romantic lake, moon and mountainside setting make this my top pick for a romantic evening. I find the food to be absolutely delicious although waaay over-presented. The plates are huge, the portions small, piled high and drizzled with colorful, exotic reductions in abstract patterns.

Menu choices are inventive. I suggest trying the local black bass, delicious! Breakfast is superb with interesting local coffee, Bodum coffee presses, linen napkins and fantastic home fried potatoes. Wines start around $30 and ascend in the direction of the stratosphere. After dinner the Havanas start at $6 and run to somewhere north of $50. This is, without doubt, the finest restaurant in the lake area. You should call for reservations. *Info: Santa Catarina Palopó. www.casapalopo.com; Tel. 502-7762-2270, 502-5773-7777.*

SANTIAGO ATITLÁN
Posada de Santiago $$
This is one of the most relaxed and tranquil lodges on the lake. There are certainly more luxurious places to stay but the Posada de Santiago is one of the most comfortable and friendly. Owner David Glanville makes you feel instantly at home. The large dining room/bar/hangout area is perfect for relaxing, checking email, talking to other travelers and playing some of the many musical instruments that are (literally) hanging around. The grounds are lush, with hundreds of coffee plants growing in the shade of huge avocado trees. The rooms range from simple doubles ($30) to large suites with fireplaces.

They also have a large room suitable for groups that frequently include film crews, students, church missions, medical volunteers, NGOs, art and yoga workshops and, of course, a few weddings. The space can be used for workshops, meetings and film presentations. Wonderful, shade grown, organic coffee is produced entirely by hand on the hotel grounds. It is delectable! Guest laundry is handled ecologically at reasonable prices.

Reba Macintyre stayed here once and Ashley Judd stopped in to use the bathroom in the restaurant.

Wi-fi is available in the restaurant. Wonderful local and international menu items tempt the palate. I particularly recommend anything they are serving that includes their smoked-on-the-premises chicken and turkey.

I don't feel comfortable in most hotels hanging around in the lobby/restaurant reading a book. At Posada de Santiago I do. *Info: Santiago de Atitlán. www.posadadesantiago.com; Tel. 502-7721-7366.*

Posada de Santiago $$

This is one of the most relaxed and tranquil lodges on the lake and they have a great restaurant, open to the public.

There is nothing too startling on the menu but you can be sure what you order will be well prepared and interesting. Fish, steak, pasta, vegetarian, Mexican and even Cajun meals are on offer. I particularly recommend anything they are serving that includes their smoked-on-the-premises chicken and turkey. Their shade grown, organic coffee is produced entirely by hand on the hotel grounds. It is delectable! *Info: Santiago de Atitlán. www.posadadesantiago.com; Tel. 502-7721-7366.*

SAN MARCOS

The village is small but boasts one bar/restaurant well worth hanging out in for a few days.

Blind Lemon's $$

Blind Lemon's restaurant/bar is cool. It was established by a blues guitarist who makes sure the weekly blues nights (Tuesdays) remain authentic. Burgers, steaks, fish and chicken are dependably good. *Info: San Marcos.*

SAN LUCAS TOLIMÁN
Hotel Toliman $$

The 20 large rooms have tile floors and are decorated with local fabrics and crafts. There's a nice pool and a fair-enough restaurant. This is not a big-time gringo tourist hotel and most of the staff do not speak English. Views are nice. *Info: San Lucas Tolimán. www.hoteltoliman.com; Tel. 502-7722-0033.*

SLEEPS & EATS

SAN MARCOS LA LAGUNA
Las Pirámides del Ka Meditation Centre $

Surrounded by lush vegetation right on the shore of the lake, the centre has two meditation temples, pyramid-shaped cabins, a library, medicinal herb garden, communal kitchen, sauna, and a vegetarian restaurant. This is a "study centre" rather than a hotel. Guests participate in daily meditation and yoga sessions. The medicinal plant sauna is a great way to start the day. Courses include meditation techniques, introduction to astral travel, vibrations or dimensions, astrology, and numerology sessions. Fasting and periods of complete silence round out the month-long moon course. One must complete the moon course before moving on to the sun course.

The facilities are basic but comfortable. The food is good but certainly not typical tourist fare. The gardens and surrounding natural beauty make this a true retreat from the stresses of civilization. The very reasonable prices include participation in study sessions. *Info: San Marcos La Laguna. www.laspiramidesdelka.com; Tel. 502-5205-7151.*

SHOPPING

BEST SHOPPING

Each village around the lake has its own style of fabrics and handicrafts. San Jorge and Santa Palopó, both near Panajachel, are known for their **woven reed mats**. San Lucas Toliman produces **hand-carved furniture**. San Pedro La Laguna produces **hand-woven rugs**. San Marcos is known for **rope and cordage** in general. Calle Santander, the main road up from the docks in Panajachel, is lined with seemingly hundreds of shops and stalls selling traditional and tourist-oriented items from all over Guatemala. The selection is awesome. Still, it is worthwhile to travel around the lake visiting the smaller towns and villages

SHOPPING

to see for yourself what is produced locally. Panajachel, San Pedro and Santiago all have shops selling things of interest to visitors but, in the smaller villages, there are few shops that you will find to be of much touristic interest.

PANAJACHEL

Panajachel has been one of the main market towns for the lake area for centuries. It still is. Dozens of small shops and even smaller stalls line **Calle Santander**, the main touristic street in town. Vendors come from all around the lake to sell their wares in Pana.

Abracadabra

Gringa owner Jerome used to sell beads and bracelets on the street here as many hippies still do. Her stuff is so nice, and her entrepreneurial instincts so strong, that she has converted her jewelry business from a street stall into the nicest jewelry store in town. Most of her offerings come from Asia but some are locally produced. I like Jerome but I try not to go into her shop. I have never been able to take a visiting lady friend into the place without a problem—I am allergic to buying jewelry. All my women

friends agree this is a great store. Guys—you have been warned.

Info: Tel. 507-209-2009.

DHL Office

Believe it or not, this is the place to buy good wine. Prices are half of what you might pay in local stores. Excellent French, Chilean and Spanish wines go mostly for under $10—a real bargain almost anywhere. The supply can be intermittent.

Info: Tel. 507-209-2009.

Bus Stop Bookshop

This is the best place to feed your reading habit. They claim to have over 4,000 titles in English, and it looks like that might be an underestimate. They have a good selection of titles covering contemporary and historical Guatemalan issues. Some of their better books are rentals.

Info: Panajachel near the intersection of Calle Santander and Calle Principal by the main bus stop.

SAN PEDRO

Not really known as a shopping destination, San Pedro

has a better selection of rolling papers in the local shops than anywhere else in the country.

SANTIAGO ATITLÁN

The street from the dock is lined with stalls and shops selling all the usual tourist stuff. No problem. The town is famous for its aggressive and persistent touts who greet all arrivals at the town dock with great enthusiasm.

BEST NIGHTLIFE & ENTERTAINMENT

Most of the villages around the lake are quite tranquil and have no real nightlife to speak of other than local cantinas. Panajachel has a great selection of nighttime activities and San Pedro has a few groovy bars.

PANAJACHEL
Watering Holes
Atlantis $$
Atlantis is a largish, dark restaurant/bar with occasional live music. They have good snacks and a couple of tables with a view of the action on the street. It does not tend to get too rowdy and loud. If you actually want to talk to the person next to you while you drink, this would be a good choice.

Info: Panajachel, Calle Santander near the top.

Live Music Venues
Sunset Café $$
If you want to enjoy the best view of the lake and the associated volcanoes while enjoying adult beverages and good sounds, Sunset Café has it. The name says it all. This is the place to be at sunset for evening drinks and live music. The beer is cold and cocktails tasty. Music runs from heavy drumming to mild rock and Latin singer/songwriter. The food is nothing to get too excited about. The service is slow. The view at any time of day or night is wonderful.

Info: Panajachel, Calle Santander near the bottom.

Pana Rock $$
With a great bar and a small bandstand, this is the best live music venue in town.

The sounds tend towards Latin-influenced rock, with local *roqueros* happily grinding out covers and some groups doing original tunes. Gringo expats reliably crank out Stevie Ray Vaughn and Eagles covers. The bar is well stocked with all your favorite, trendy tipples and the bartenders are attentive, friendly and capable of whipping up some interesting umbrella drinks, if you must.

Info: Panajachel, about in the middle of Calle Santander.

Circus Bar $$
This is an intimate, dark and low-ceilinged, lively spot to spend an evening enjoying live flamenco guitar and other sounds. It can get crowded and boisterous at times but most nights it's just a quiet crowd digging the music, food and fine beverages. The beer is cold, the pizza cheesy and the crowd appreciative of the musicians. The quality of the music varies from night to night but it's almost always great. This is the most dependable spot in town for good live music. One of the usual musicians is rumored to have spent time playing with the Gypsy Kings. Expect

to hear some straight ahead flamenco, old school bolero, trova and some plain old Latin standards. I like to stick my head in the door once or twice a night to see who's on. I often wind up staying for an hour or three and a beer or four.

Info: Panajachel, just past the top of Calle Santander.

SANTIAGO ATITLÁN
Once you're in Santiago you should forget about Panajachel and its nightlife. Pana seems like downtown Manhattan after a few days in tranquil Santiago. It's about a 45-minute boat ride across the lake and boats stop running about 5:30. You can contract with a boat to take you back after dark but it's cheaper just to rent a room and stay.

Posada de Santiago has live music most weekend nights and often during the week.

SAN PEDRO LA LAGUNA
Watering Holes
La Piscina San Pedro is a good spot to waste an afternoon soaking up the sun while enjoying cold beverages. They have a nice pool, bocce, table games, pretty good bar and

bar food. The location by the Santiago docks affords a wonderful view; which is one of the main reasons to be here.

Info: By the Santiago dock. Tel. 502-5911-1481.

BEST SPORTS & RECREATION

Active travelers will find Lake Atitlán to be a good base for scuba diving, hang gliding, kayaking, volcano hiking, and on and on for a long list of sweat-inducing activities.

Motorbike & Scooter Rentals
Panajachel has one place where you can rent a small scooter, larger motorcycle, tuk-tuk, car and anything in between, **Mako Moto Rent**. I rented a Honda Civic from them and drove it all over the place: Tikal, Cobán, Ixtapa.

Info: Cerca de Avenida Los Arboles. Tel. 502-7762-1192, 502-7762-2089. They will want a deposit, credit card and passport. Ask for "Mako."

Paragliding
Indisputably the King of the Skies in Guatemala, Roger Lapointe, based in Panajachel, is the man to see. He has been teaching, coaching and tandem flying (yes, he will fly with you strapped in!) over the lake for 8 years.

He can arrange for transportation, lodging and week-long training sessions in one of the most beautiful places in the world to soar like a bird.

Info: www.paragliding guatemala.com; Tel. 502-5595-7732.

Fishing
Believe it or not, bass fishing is quite good on the lake. This is the same bass that rednecks

SPORTS & RECREATION

VOLCANO WALK

Since these are usually much more *hikes* than walks, unless you're young and fit (you know who you are) go ahead, rent the horse. But do it at the beginning, not halfway up. Buy the walking stick from the little kid. You'll need it too. I suggest heavy leather work gloves to help scramble over the sharp lava rocks.

(and myself) in the Southern US spend thousands chasing around in high-powered bass boats. They grow to over 20 lbs. in the approximately 1,500 depths of the lake. **Martin Chif** owns a local gas station and provides boats and all the tackle you need to haul in a lunker. Take a camera. Your buddies back in Arkansas will not believe you. The best time is late afternoon, and he takes two people out for about $75.

Info: Tel. 502-7721-7363.

Sailing Tours
In Santiago, Ian has a 22-foot sailing cruiser, and knows all the scenic and peaceful places on the lake for a day of gunkholing. Food and wine are available. Just getting to the area usually involves a

water taxi or ferry but the lake is so beautiful that most visitors hope for more time on the water to absorb the stunning scenery.

Info: Tel. 502-5464-0204.

Kayaking
Kayaking anywhere on the lake is a mystic experience. The beauty and awesome energy of the surrounding volcanoes are intensified many times when you are sitting quietly in a kayak a couple of hundred feet from shore. This is a *you've gotta do it* thing to do. Within five minutes paddling from the beach in Pana, you will find yourself in another world.

Just head west from the beach along the shore and head for the extremely ugly high-rise hotel **La Riviera de Atitlán**. You can't miss it. Just before you get to it you will pass by and admire the lovely **Hotel Atitlán**. When you are right in front of the Riviera de Atitlán it looks much better for some reason. Keep going along the shore for a little and you will pass some reeds. At this point, you can slowly cut across the bay back to the east back past the ferry boats towards the beach. You can easily complete this trip in a leisurely hour. Take two hours. Kayaks are easily rented by the hour from a stand near the beach a little past Posada de Don Rodrigo.

For about $3-$4 per hour you can rent basic sit-on kayaks with paddle and lifejacket at **Diverciones Acuaticas Balam**. Thye have a couple of tandems and some sit-ons as well. The owner has small lockers you can use to store things you don't want to get wet, like your shoes. If you are hard-core, call him and he'll open up for you at any crazy hour in the morning you like. They also have water skiing.

Info: On the beach in Panajachel. Tel. 502- 7762-2242.

Hiking & Horesback Riding
Guided hikes and horseback rides through the communities and forests around the lake can be arranged by expatriates **Jim and Nancy Matison**. They can do half- or full-day hikes with lunch. The hikes can be tailored to your physical strengths and interests.

Info: Tel. 502-5811-5516, 502-5742-8975.

Culturally Significant Tours
Santiago is filthy with history and interesting sites. Much Mayan culture remains, and ruins of colonial architecture is everywhere. The local inhabitants, mostly **Tz'utujil Mayans**, have preserved much of their culture and have created an interesting fusion of the imposed European customs and their own ancient traditions. Do not miss a visit to the tomb/shrine of Maximón, a sort of Catholic deity who avidly accepts offerings of booze and cigarettes: you get the idea.

Easter-related activities span an entire week. Processions, kite flying, masked dances, mock crucifixions and other colorful ceremonies too complicated for me to understand abound. Lodging is a problem anywhere in Guatemala during Easter Week.

For colorful and educational walking tours through the town of Santiago, **Dolores Ratzán** (*Tel. 502-5730-4570*) speaks excellent English and has expert knowledge of Tz'utujil culture and customs,

SPORTS & RECREATION

WEAVING LESSONS

If you really, really admire the local, astoundingly-bright local fabrics, you can schedule a weaving lesson with **Concepción Ratzán Mendoza** (*Santiago de Atitlán, Tel. 502-7721-7409*). In three to six hours she can help you produce a 12" x 32" piece of colorful cloth, hopefully resembling the beautiful things you see local women wearing and for sale in markets. The price for the lesson and materials is about $25—a real bargain.

particularly its folk Catholicism. She takes guests to all the churches, historical sites and finishes her 2-hour tours with a visit to a weaving workshop and, if you like, to the market and handicraft stalls to help you purchase local handicrafts and art. The tour runs about $40 for four people.

Amanda Chif (*Tel. 502-7721-7363*), a former Peace Corps volunteer, will take you on a tour on a tuk-tuk (small, three-wheeled taxi-like conveyance) to all the sites in and around town. This is a safe and relaxing way for those of us with failing knees, etc. to get to the local sites.

The Nature Reserve at **San Buena Ventura de Atitlán** covers 400 acres and serves as a refuge for the flora, birds, insects and small animals of the area. They have self-guided interpreted nature trails with a twelve-page guide printed in English and Spanish. The huge, enclosed butterfly garden boasts over 30 species of native Guatemalan butterflies. Recently, they have developed unobtrusive trails through their formerly closed-off, protected bird refuge. The walks include elevated walkways, tree platforms, and suspension bridges. Bird sustenance plantings include over 250 native fruit trees and over 3,000 native flowering and seed-bearing plants. The orchid exhibition includes more than 50 of the more than 500 native species. Unfortunately, they also include an eight-platform zipline. They offer guides.

Info: Tel. 502-7762-2565.

6. CHICHICASTENANGO

HIGHLIGHTS

▲ Procession up the Santo Tomás steps

▲ Mayan Inn – quaint colonial architecture

▲ Shop for your favorite fabrics – one of the biggest handicraft markets in Central America

▲ Sample homemade tamales – Colorful Mayan women sell fresh tamales and other goodies from baskets on their heads

COORDINATES

Chichi is a highland market town located a few miles off the Intercontinental highway a few hours west of Guatemala City. It is a gateway to the Verapaces Highlands.

INTRO

The enormous **Sunday market at Chichicastenango** is often billed as "the most colorful market in Central America". It probably is, but it's more than just brilliant fabrics and picture-postcard vegetable stalls. It's a special place and time that incorporates the beauty of daily market life with the rituals of the Catholic Church and local **K'iche' Mayan** culture. Clouds of incense, enormously loud fireworks and awesome **Cofradía** processions, with Mayan women dressed to the nines in their traditional hand woven fabrics, combine to produce, understandably, one of the **top tourist draws in Guatemala**. Oh yeah, there are hordes of tourists jostling about through the acres of crafts stalls and vegetable stands pushing their cameras out in front of them like so many Christians on a pilgrimage holding out bibles. It's a blast. I love the Sunday market at Chichi.

ONE GREAT DAY IN CHICHI

The main, if not only, reason to come to Chichicastenango is to wander through the huge, spectacularly colorful local market and gawk at the **Cofradía processions**. There is no need to stay longer than a few hours. **Market days are Thursday and Sunday**. Sunday markets are usually larger and, on Sundays of particular significance, loud, crazily-costumed, almost wild religious processions thread their way through the crowds. It's very cool.

Arrive midmorning, wander the market, visit the two churches, eat lunch at the lovely Mayan Inn or at one of the market stalls, wander the market again in the afternoon (this time buying things), and leave around 2pm in the afternoon, missing the worst of the exiting traffic.

Morning

Several transportation companies like Tierra Maya offer round trips to Chichi twice a week in tourist shuttle vans from Guatemala City, Antigua and Panajachel. This is an easy and convenient way to see

SIGHTS

the market. It is best to arrive midmorning, say around 10. Step one is to carefully remember exactly where your ride is parked. Parking touts abound. Wander through the market aimlessly at first, enjoying the colorful scene. I suggest having a good look around for an hour or so before making any purchases. That way you get a chance to see what is available and, maybe, get an idea of what the prices are. Walk up the steps of both churches and have a look inside (no photos inside). Wait for the procession to come up the steps of **Santo Tomás** in dramatic fashion (*see photo at right*).

The church was built on the site of a pre-Columbian Mayan temple. Mayan priests still perform ceremonies here. This is the place where the oldest known copy of the Mayan bible, the **Popul Vuh**, was found. There are 18 steps, corresponding to the 18 months in the Mayan Calendar. Take lots of photos and be sure to tip everyone in sight.

I like to sit quietly on the church steps, just above the ladies selling flowers and in-

cense, watching the show go by below me. This is a great spot to take pictures. It's easy to take hundreds of shots in an hour or so. If you pick your spot right, you will have a good view as the processioners, worshippers and other assorted strangely-costumed Cofradía participants do their thing. You may choke on incense but you will see a wonderful show.

Afternoon
Even if you don't plan on eating lunch there, take a walk through the beautiful gardens and public areas of the lovely and quaint **Mayan Inn**. Ad-

SIGHTS

mire the centuries-old buildings. Marvel at the huge wooden ceiling beams.

After lunch go back to wandering the market but with an eye to actually buying the trinkets or treasures you have had your eye on all day. Make your purchase(s), find where your ride is parked and, about 2pm or so, fight the traffic out of town. What a day! Great photos, great shopping, plenty to gawk at, Chichicastenango is just an all around good touristic day out.

One of the most famous shopping destinations in Central America, the Thursday and Sunday markets at Chichi are a famous riot of color, an interesting mix of traditional Mayan people rubbing shoulders with gringo tourist hordes amid raucous religious processions. Some feel this is the only place to do your shop-

ping. Realize, however, that the market draws literally thousands of free spending tourists, most of them not particularly good at bargaining. This can cause prices to trend upward. Many feel selections are as good or better in Antigua and particularly, Panajachel.

I have heard it said that the best time to buy at Chichi is in the middle of the afternoon, around 2pm or so, when many vendors will be facing a long ride home with lots of unsold merchandise. The idea is that they may be willing to sell for a bit less at the end of the day. From what I can see, almost all of the vendors have an absolutely huge amount of inventory. I doubt if any of the vendors selling tourist items sell even 10% of their stock on a given market day. The guys selling belts have hundreds of them. The people selling masks have hundreds of them. I doubt that the prospect of hauling home one or two fewer pieces of cloth at the end of the day is going to cause many of the vendors to drop their prices significantly.

My suggestion is to spend an hour or so wandering around

the market area in general (it only covers 4 or 5 blocks) to get an idea for how much the items you are interested in buying are being sold for and what different qualities are available. Then go back just after lunch to make your purchases. The market is very crowded and walk spaces are quite narrow. You won't want to be schlepping around bulky purchases all day.

Eat lunch either in a market stall restaurant or at the **Mayan Inn**. All sorts of interesting things to eat are on offer in the market from stalls with actual chairs, or from a basket on top of a Mayan lady's head. Weird fruits, soups, roasted meats, tacos, fried chicken and, the best of all to me, homemade tamales. If you can find a lady with a basket of tamales on top of her head, you should buy one or two, unwrap the corn husks, put on a little hot sauce and dig into some of the best street eats anywhere.

SIGHTS

7. TIKAL

HIGHLIGHTS

▲ Grand Plaza – Twin pyramids form a plaza with dozens of stelae and altars

▲ Temple of the Great Jaguar – built by King Au Cacao

▲ Temple of the Two-headed Serpent – the tallest existing Mayan structure

▲ Morely Museum – displays of ceramic and jade artifacts

COORDINATES

Tikal is located in Petén province in the northern, most heavily forested part of the country. The nearby towns of **El Remate** and **Flores** offer a wide choice of tourist facilities. You can fly here quite easily. is easy to get around, and stupefies the imagination with its hundreds of huge, exotic structures. Who built them?

INTRO

Tikal National Park is the world's largest excavated Mayan site. Surrounded by dense rainforest, the enormous pyramids of Tikal only hint at what used to be the Mayan Los Angeles. The park, although sprawling,

🚶 A WEEKEND IN TIKAL

It's possible, although a bit hurried, to visit Tikal on a day trip from Guatemala City, but it really deserves at least an overnight trip. It's a very large and spread-out site, so you're going to do a lot of walking if you want to see even half of it. Also, many feel it would be a shame not to be there early in the morning, when the site is shrouded in that mysterious jungle mist, and you're more likely to see some of the birds and other wildlife that abound around the site.

Fly in directly from Guatemala City, spend the night on Lake Petén Itzá and be at the park gates first thing in the morning for the famous mysterious jungle mist.

Friday Evening
You can fly to the Guatema-

lan town of Flores from Guatemala City, or take a bus or rental car directly to Tikal National Park. However you get here, call in advance to reserve a room at one of the nice hotels near Remate around **Lake Petén Itzá**, close

SIGHTS

SIGHTS

to the park. My favorite is **La Lancha**, a small, quiet boutique hotel. It has a pool that's going to feel very good after trudging around the ruins all day. There are three hotels right by the park entrance but they are of poor quality, suffering from waaay too much tourist traffic. I cannot recommend any of them.———

If you get there early enough, drop by the visitors' center and line up a guide for next morning. It's well worth paying a few bucks to learn about the history of the site, and it's always a good thing to support the local economy. Take a guided tour tomorrow morning, then wander about on your own the rest of the day.

Speaking of that pool, it may just be time for a dip and a cold beer, then dinner at your hotel restaurant. There's no big nightlife scene around here, but the hotel bars often harbor some lively conversation among the visitors from all over the world.

Saturday Morning
The name Tikal means **"Place of Voices."** The voices of the ancient Mayans speak most clearly early in the morning,

so you might want to be there right at 6am when the gates open. Early morning mist rises from the jungle, revealing the huge stone heads of long-dead kings. Ceiba roots entwine the stones, flocks of colorful parrots flit about, and deer graze irreverently among the ancient palaces.

By late morning, the hot tropical sun has burned off the mist, and the deer are replaced by herds of irreverent gringos, each clad in ball cap and t-shirt, with an ice cream cone in one hand and a water bottle firmly clutched in the other. It's not possible to evade them altogether (you may, like me, actually *be* one), but if you time your visit just right, you can avoid the midday rush.

During the Maya's Classic Period (around 300-900 AD), Tikal was one of the largest and most powerful city-states in the Mayan world, a metropolis of over 100,000 residents that traded with cultures as far away as Teotihuacan in Mexico, and made war with neighbors such as Caracol and Naranjo. Rulers such as **Dark Sun, Stormy Sky** and **Jaguar Paw** built grand palaces, temples

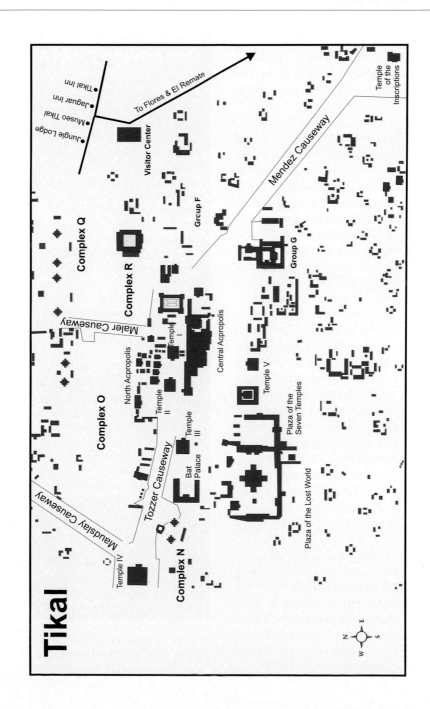

SIGHTS

and monuments, and recorded their deeds in the Mayan glyphs on stelae (stone columns).

Archaeological work at the site began in 1882, but only a fraction of the city of Tikal has yet been excavated. Don't worry though, even that fraction will be enough to keep you stomping about all day: over 3,000 structures, including six large pyramids, 250 stelae, several royal palaces, no less than seven ball courts and hundreds of small residential buildings. The centerpiece is the **Grand Plaza**, where two pyramids, the Temple of the Great Jaguar and the Temple of the Masks, face each other with a large plaza in between, surrounded by dozens of stelae and altars. Around the corner is the complex called the **Lost World**, with a huge pyramid and other structures from several different historical periods.

Visiting Tikal is a good workout, as it is an enormous site. It's no place to visit with small children, or anyone who minds walking. The walk from the entrance to the Grand Plaza is almost a mile. Raised causeways connect other sec-

THE ANCIENT MAYA

During their **Golden Age** (300-900 AD), the Mayans built a highly advanced empire that extended from Mexico through Guatemala and Belize to Honduras. Their calendar and knowledge of astronomy were unequalled until modern times. Their monumental ceremonial sites were the scenes of **elaborate rituals**, including human sacrifice. Although Mayans continue to live in the area today, their advanced civilization collapsed before the Spanish arrived. The exact reasons for their demise are a mystery, but most scientists agree that climate change and droughts did them in. Some believe that poor stewardship of the environment played a role (sound familiar?). With its wealth of Mayan sites, Guatemala is an excellent place to explore the history of this fascinating people. To learn more, see:

- www.mayaruins.com
- www.mayan-world.com
- www.mayaweb.nl
- www.lost-civilizations.net
- www.mesoweb.com
- www.gomaya.com

tions of the city. It's another long walk to the **Temple of the Two-headed Serpent**, at

230 feet the tallest Mayan structure in the world. You'll really get a workout as you scramble to the top of the partially excavated pyramid, to be rewarded with a spectacular panorama of the surrounding jungle. The trails that connect the various parts of the site make for a pleasant hike through the jungle. Parrots, toucans, spider and howler monkeys are common, and the partially cleared landscape makes spotting them easier than in the dense jungle.

Saturday Afternoon
When the midday heat starts becoming oppressive, you can amble back to the hotel if you are staying at one of the on-site hotels and cool off with a quick dip in the pool, then try one of the small *comedores* across from the visitors' center for a Guatemalan lunch. After lunch, visit the two small museums at the site. The

ALTERNATE PLAN
Lakefront **Santa Elena** is a typically chaotic and colorful little Guatemalan town, and adjacent **Flores** is quite a pleasant tourist-oriented town on a little island in the lake.

Morley Museum, named for a colorful character who was one of the early explorers, displays beautiful ceramic and jade artifacts from the site. At the visitors' center, the most interesting of Tikal's stelae are protected.

In this climate, it makes sense to get up early, and do your walking around before it gets really hot. You might even indulge in that civilized Spanish/Latin American custom called a *siesta*, and nap for a couple of hours in the afternoon. In the evening, you can go back into the park for another hour or so, perhaps seeing the **Palace of the Inscriptions**.

Info: Tikal National Park is open daily 6am-6pm. Entry is $20, which includes the Morley Museum. www.tikalpark.com.

Saturday Evening
The park normally closes at 6pm, but we have heard that on full-moon nights, you can get a special ticket to go in at night – surely a spiritual and spooky experience! Otherwise, it's another night of drinking beer or rum and swapping travel stories at the hotel bar.

SIGHTS

SIGHTS

Sunday

If you get going fairly early, you'll have time for a little side trip on the way back to Guatemala City (or, if you haven't had your fill of the Mayans, you could certainly spend another morning at Tikal).

More Tikal ...

Tikal is the world's largest excavated Mayan site. Today it's a **UNESCO World Heritage Site**, and Guatemala's most popular national park.

Some of Tikal's monuments have been dated as far back as the fourth century BC. During the Maya's **Classic Period** (around 300-900 AD), Tikal was one of the largest and most powerful city-states in the Mayan world, a metropo-lis of over 100,000 residents that traded with cultures as far away as Teotihuacan in Mexico, and a military power that made war with neighbors such as Caracol and Naranjo.

During the Maya's **Early Classic Period**, Tikal was the dominant power in the region, led by rulers such as Dark Sun, Stormy Sky and Jaguar Paw, who built a fine palace that survives today. Around 562 AD however, Tikal lost a lengthy war with nearby Caracol. This was followed by a century or so when no large monuments were built at Tikal, a period researchers call the "Tikal Hiatus," and which divides Mayan history into the Early and Late Classic periods. In 182 AD, the ruler

Jasaw Chan K'awiil I (or Ah Cacau) and his queen Lady Twelve Macaw began to restore Tikal's former glory, defeating Calakmul in a bloody battle in 711. Later rulers built the city's most impressive temples and tombs, the Maya declined and Tikal was abandoned by the end of the 10th century.

Tikal was mentioned in John Lloyd Stephen's 1841 book *Incidents of Travel in Central America, Chiapas and Yucatan*, and the first scientific expedition arrived in 1848. In 1882, Sir Arthur Percival Maudslay began clearing forest, and made the first drawings and photos of the site. Other important early researchers were Teobert Mahler and Sylvanus Morley (a fascinating character whose archaeological travels provided cover for his WWI espionage activities). The raised causeways that connect sections of the city have been named for some of the important researchers.

Even after many years of work, only a fraction of the city of Tikal has yet been excavated. That fraction however, is so large that a long day is barely enough time to see it all. Archaeologists have found over 3,000 structures, including six large pyramids, 250 stelae, several royal palaces, no less than seven ball courts, hundreds of small residential homes and even a building that seems to have been a jail. The centerpiece of the city is the **Grand Plaza**. Here two pyramids face each other with a large plaza in between, one of several sets of twin pyramids at Tikal. The **Temple of the Great Jaguar** was built by the king Ah Cacau around 700 AD, and contains his tomb. The **Temple of the Masks**, named for the carved faces on its lintel, was built for his queen (naturally it's a little smaller). The Grand Plaza is an enormous and very complex site in itself, with a huge palace and dozens of stelae and altars.

Around the corner from the Grand Plaza is an area called El Mundo Perdido, or the **Lost World**, a large complex centered on an enormous pyramid. Here are all kinds of sinister structures, including the Temple of the Skulls, and a mysterious tunnel with an entrance shaped like the mouth of a snake. The inter-

SIGHTS

esting thing about this complex is that you can see structures from several different historical periods, which is unusual, as the Mayans usually built new temples on top of older ones.

A good walk along the Tozzer Causeway brings you to the **Temple of the Two-headed Serpent**, at 230 feet the tallest existing Mayan structure. It was built by the ruler Yik'in Chan Kawil in 741 AD. The pyramid is only partially excavated, so it's a hardscrabble climb to the top, but the physically fit will be rewarded with a spectacular panorama of the surrounding jungle. In fact, you'd better be pretty fit to visit Tikal, as it is an enormous site. The walk from the entrance to the Grand Plaza is almost a mile, and you'll walk many miles by the time you've seen most of it. Walking the trails that connect the various parts of the site is quite pleasant (but hot), as the jungle grows all around and within the park. You'll see huge ceiba (*kapok*) trees, which were sacred to the Maya, as well as mahogany and sapodilla (*chicle*). Spider and howler monkeys are common, and coatis and other

small mammals are not rare. Don't stand below monkeys in trees!

Birding is wonderful here— parrots, toucans and other rarer species abound, the partially cleared landscape makes spotting them easy, and the pyramids make splendid viewing platforms.

There are two small museums at the site. The **Morley Museum** displays beautiful ceramic and jade artifacts from the site. At the visitors' center, the most interesting of Tikal's stelae are protected. Adjacent to the park are three hotels, a campground and a few small *comedores*.

Info: www.tikalpark.com. Tikal National Park is open daily 6am-6pm. Entry is $20, which includes the Morley Museum.

BEST SLEEPS & EATS

There are three lodges on the grounds of the park itself: **Jungle Lodge, Tikal Inn** and **Jaguar Inn**. The Jaguar Inn is more of a hostel. I can only weakly recommend two of them, and the Jungle Lodge I can't recommend at all. The nicest, the Tikal Inn, has reasonably nice rooms and a wonderful pool. It's fairly quiet and jungly. However, the service is surly and the food barely passable. The service staffs' eyes have that glazed look they get when they have seen *waaay* too many tour-bus loads of tourists being herded through.

There are also some nice hotels in the town of Flores, but it's 45 minutes away. **El Remate** and the area around **Lake Petén Itzá** are a little closer and have several interesting lodging options. The wonderful La Lancha, Francis Ford Coppola's joint, is handy enough. The Camino Real is the nicest upscale option.

The Tikal Inn $$
This is the nicest of the three lodging options at the park, because it has a pool. The rooms are nothing fancy, but they are clean and comfortable enough. All have private bath and ceiling fans. The pool is quite nice, and believe me, you will appreciate it after trudging around the ruins in the jungle humidity. *Info: www.tikalinn.com; Tel. 502-7926-1917.*

The Jaguar Inn $$
Next door to the Tikal Inn, the Jaguar has similar rooms at about the same price (50-60 bucks for a double room). Each of these hotels has a restaurant and bar.
Info: www.jaguartikal.com; Tel. 502-7926-0002.

SLEEPS & EATS

BEST OF THE BEST NEAR TIKAL

La Lancha $$$$

Francis Ford Coppola's joint is a little further out the crummy road on the lake and is still handy enough for easy visits to the

park. It is a 10-room boutique hotel with local furniture and colorful fabrics everywhere. Big hammocks and comfortable spots to hang out are plentiful. There is a pool and the lake is a short walk away. "Gourmet" Guatemalan dishes are served in the restaurant. *Info: www.blancaneaux.com; Tel. 502-7928-8331.*

Camino Real Tikal $$$$

For most, this is the nicest upscale option in the Tikal area. It is

an international resort chain-style hotel with two restaurants, bars, coffee shop, pool, sailing, kayaking, and free shuttle from the airport. There is a tropical feel with palm trees, thatched roofs and colorful umbrella drinks. The restaurant food is fine, which is good since there is nowhere else to eat nearby. *Info: www.caminoreal.com.gt; Tel. 502-2333-3000.*

Hotel Ecologico Finca Ixobel $

Half way between Río Dulce and Flores south of Poptún, this is a real gem and a good place to spend the night if you are driving to or from Guatemala City. It's tranquil and laid back, the rooms are comfortable, and the common areas are friendly. Help yourself to drinks and snacks. Dinners are served buffet style. The hotel features a wonderful bakery, so be ready to add a couple of pounds. The bungalows are a real bargain. The guests tend towards younger, experienced travelers with plenty of time. *Info: South of Poptún. www.fincaixobel.com; Tel. 502-5410-4307.*

In addition to the hotel restaurants (very bad), there's a generic tourist café at the visitors' center, and a couple of cheaper and slightly more interesting *comedores* across the street. They aren't very good either, but are half the price of the hotel restaurants.

BEST SHOPPING

There is some shopping of note in **Flores** but the selections are thin compared to what you will see in Antigua, Panajachel or Chichicastenango. Imitation Mayan artifacts are the only real local products.

SHOPPING

8. COPÁN EXCURSION

HIGHLIGHTS
▲ Mayan Ruins of Copán – once the bustling capital of a highly advanced civilization

▲ The town of Copán Ruinas – a quaint and friendly colonial town

▲ The Villages of the Lenca Trail – a perfect climate, classic colonial architecture, and the finest handicrafts in Honduras

COORDINATES

Copán is located just a few miles over the border from Guatemala in **Honduras**. The closest town is **Copán Ruinas**. It is an easy half-day journey from Guatemala City.

INTRO

The **Mayan Ruins** of **Copán** are just a hop, skip, and a jump over the border in Honduras. The exotic sculptures and other art treasures make it arguably the most interesting of all the world's Mayan sites. The quaint village of Copán Ruinas is a tourist hub, and there are all sorts of attractions in the area.

🚶 A DAY IN COPÁN

Copán is one of the few places in Honduras where tourist facilities are quite well developed. You should have little trouble dropping in for a day. There are plenty of bus (and now, air) connections from Guatemala City. Plan ahead with a local tour operator and you can see the highlights of the ruins in a day.

Morning
The **Mayan Ruins of Copán** are one of the most important cultural monuments in the world. One of the largest excavated Mayan sites, Copán was a **cultural capital**, and is richer in sculptures, hieroglyphics and art treasures than any other known Mayan site.

Copán is just 7 miles (12 km) from the Guatemalan border, and the road that passes

Copán is the main route between the two countries. If you're traveling overland to or from **Guatemala City**, this is the route you'll take.

Check for day trips. It's 7-8 hours by bus between Guatemala City and Copán Ruinas. The border is open daily 7am-5pm.

Monarcas Travel (www.angelfire.com/mt/monarcastravel; Tel. 502-7832-1939 in Guatemala) and **Atitrans** (www.atitrans.com; Tel. 502/7832-3371 or 502/7831-0184 in Guatemala) each offer minivan service to Copán from Antigua and Guatemala City for about $30-37.

To get the most from your visit, I recommend taking a guided tour, which you can

SIGHTS

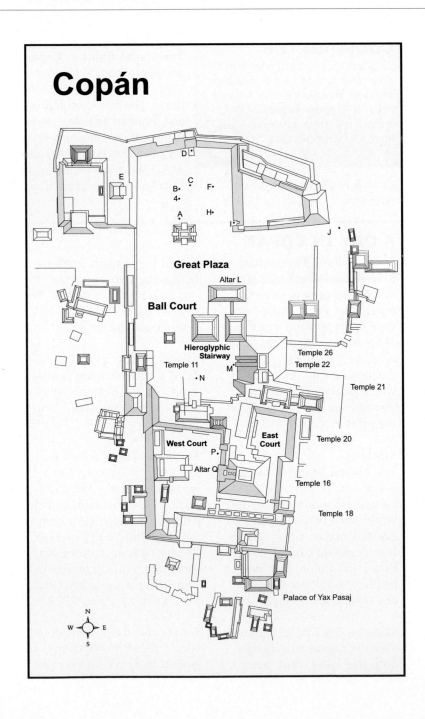

Copán

D

E

B
4

C

F

A

H

I

J

Great Plaza

Altar L

Ball Court

**Hieroglyphic
Stairway**

Temple 11

N

M

Temple 26

Temple 22

Temple 21

West Court

P

East
Court

Temple 20

Altar Q

Temple 16

Temple 18

Palace of Yax Pasaj

N
W — E
S

arrange at the visitors' center. The **Copán Guide Association** (Tel. 504-651-4018) offers tours of the ruins, starting at $20.

Info: Entry to the park is $10, which also includes the Sepulturas archaeological site. Entry to the Museum of Mayan Sculpture is $5. The park and the Sculpture Museum are open daily 8am-4pm.

As you explore the sights of Copán, your guide will tell you the fascinating story of the highly advanced Mayan civilization and the ceremonial site of Copán.

The **Great Plaza** features elaborately-carved stelae and altars featuring images of Mayan rulers and gods, with hieroglyphic inscriptions. Back in the golden age of the Maya (300-900 AD), the stelae, and many of the buildings, were painted in bright colors, traces of which can still be seen here and there.

At the **Ball Court**, the Mayans played a game that involved putting a hard **rubber** ball through a stone hoop without using their hands. Apparently

STELAE

A **stele** (plural stelae) is a standing stone slab, generally erected to commemorate an event such as the reign of a ruler. Many stelae feature images and glyphs carved in relief. Most were originally painted with bright colors.

they took it almost as seriously as today's Latin Americans do their soccer—some believe that the losers provided the human sacrifices that were supposed to appease the gods.

Towering 100 feet over the Great Plaza, the **Acropolis** is a large complex of pyramids and temples that was built over many earlier temples.

SIGHTS

Here are the beautiful **Rosalila Temple**, or Temple of the Sun, painted in rose-lilac colors, and the **Plaza of the Jaguars**, with its rich carvings depicting Maya beliefs about the afterworld.

The **Hieroglyphic Stairway** has 63 steps, carved with 1,500 intricate glyphs, the longest known text left by the ancient Mayans. It is believed to be an official chronology of all the rulers of Copán, telling the history of their great battles and deeds.

Unless you're really into archaeology, skip the optional visit to the **tunnels**. It costs an extra $12, and is only slightly interesting.

Afternoon
There's a cafeteria-style restaurant right on site, but it serves exactly the sort of generic tourist feed you'd expect of a place squarely in the center of the beaten path. However, you're trying to see a lot in one day, so refuel with an overpriced burger for now.

The **Museum of Mayan Sculpture**, adjacent to the ruins, costs an extra five bucks, but it's worth every Lempira. Many of the original art treasures of Copán are displayed here in the museum, protected from the elements, while the *in situ* versions are actually clever replicas. Surprise!

The centerpiece of the museum is a life-size replica of the Rosalila Temple, in all its original pink splendor. The collection of Mayan sculpture is the finest in the world.

If there's time, have another stroll through the ruins after you've seen the museum. I think you'll find it quite interesting to take a second look now that you know a bit about the history of the city.

A WEEKEND IN COPÁN

There are plenty of interesting sights around Copán. A weekend gives you just enough time to devote a good solid day to the ruins, hike in the beautiful countryside, and spend some time hanging out in the town of **Copán Ruinas**. But beware – once you get a taste of how much there is to do around here, you'll wish you had more time.

Friday

Show up in Copán Ruinas Friday evening and scope out the scene. The first stop is the **Tunkul Bar and Restaurant**, for a cold beer and a chat with the staff about what's going on in the area. The in-house **Go Native Tours** (*Tel. 504-651-4410*) is only one of a dozen tour operators in town, offering trips to Mayan sites, cloud forests, coffee farms, Lenca villages and all sorts of other fascinating sights in the region. Another option is **Yaragua Tours** (*Tel. 504-651-4147*). For your tour of the ruins tomorrow morning, simply call the **Copán Guide Association** at the park (*Tel. 504-651-4018*).

With your plans for tomorrow all sorted, think about dinner. Copán Ruinas has several very nice possibilities, including healthy and delicious fare at **Twisted Tanya's**, or hearty grilled meats with a nice river view at **Carnitas Nía Lola**.

Copán Ruinas goes to bed pretty early, and you should probably do the same, because you will want to get up bright and early for a visit to the ruins. There are good lodg-

ing options in all price ranges, from the elegant **Hotel Marina Copán** to the cozy **Casa de Café**.

Saturday

After a breakfast of sweet and juicy tropical fruit and rich Honduran coffee, head to the park in plenty of time to be the first through the gates at 8am, so you'll have an hour or two to enjoy the ruins in relative peace, before the flood of day-trippers arrives. Early birds may see deer grazing among the ancient palaces in the morning mist. By late morning, the sun has burned off the mist, and the deer are replaced by herds of gringos with their ball caps, t-shirts and water bottles.

SIGHTS

The Mayan Ruins of Copán are one of the most important cultural monuments in the world, and have been designated a **UNESCO World Heritage Site**. Copán is one of the three largest and most famous excavated Mayan sites. Copán was a **cultural capital**, and is richer in sculptures, hieroglyphics and art treasures than any other known Mayan site. It has also been the subject of more research than any other Mayan city. Because of the **wealth of hieroglyphics**, Copán has been an invaluable source of information for scientists researching the ancient Mayan civilization.

During their golden age (300-900 AD) the Mayan empire extended from southern Mexico through Guatemala, Belize and El Salvador to western Honduras. The Mayans developed a highly advanced civilization – their calendar and their knowledge of astronomy were unequalled until modern times. Copán's golden age began in 553 with the ruler **Moon Jaguar**, who built the spectacular Rosalila Temple. Other prominent potentates were **Smoke Imix**, who built many stelae and temples, **18 Rab-**bit, who built the Great Plaza and the Ball Court, **Smoke Shell**, who built the famous Hieroglyphic Stairway, and **Yax Pac**, who built Altar Q, which depicts all of Copán's rulers up to that point.

Sometime during the 9th century AD, the grand city of Copán was abandoned. While it sounds romantic to say that "no one knows why," in fact modern scientists have a pretty good idea of why the Mayan civilization collapsed. The ancient Mayans cleared large areas of forest for agriculture, but the soil proved surprisingly poor for growing crops, so as the population grew, they kept clearing more and more land. The **deforestation** led to erosion, making the land even less able to support decent crop yields. In the end they simply couldn't grow enough food to feed themselves, and the population went into a long decline, until the Maya had dwindled to scattered bands of hunter-gatherers and farmers.

Unfortunately, history is currently repeating itself in Honduras. In many parts of the country, **slash-and-burn agriculture** has denuded whole regions, leaving the poor subsistence farmers unable to make a living. Forced to leave their homes, they move into more remote areas and repeat the process there. The Honduran government is making a valiant effort to conserve some of the rain forest, but they simply don't have the resources to stop the destruction.

It's food for thought as you explore the sights of Copán. The **Great Plaza** is a large open space dotted with stelae and altars featuring bas-relief statues of Mayan rulers and gods, with hieroglyphic inscriptions. Back in the day, the stelae, and many of the buildings, were painted in bright colors, traces of which can still be seen here and there. Most of the stelae in the Great Plaza are believed to have been built around AD 710-740 by the ruler 18 Rabbit.

South of the Great Plaza is the **Ball Court**, decorated with images of macaws, which were sacred birds. Here the Mayans played a game that involved putting a hard rubber ball through a stone hoop without using their hands.

Some believe that the losers provided the human sacrifices that were supposed to appease the gods.

Towering 100 feet over the Great Plaza, the **Acropolis** is a large complex of pyramids and temples that was built over many earlier temples. Here are the beautiful **Rosalila Temple**, or Temple of the Sun, painted in rose-lilac colors, as well as the **Plaza of the Jaguars**, with its rich carvings depicting Maya beliefs about the afterworld.

The tallest structure at the site is the **Hieroglyphic Stairway**, built in AD 749 by the ruler Smoke Shell. The 63 steps are carved with 1,500 glyphs, the longest known text left by the ancient Mayans. It is believed to be a chronology of all the rulers of Copán, telling the history of their great battles and deeds. The stairway has provided archaeologists with some important missing links in the city's history.

One of the most interesting artworks at Copán is **Altar Q**, which was built by one of the city's last leaders, Yax Pac. It depicts all 16 of Copán's rulers up to that point, with Yax

SIGHTS

K'uk'Mo' handing the symbolic baton of kingship over to Yax Pac.

The archaeologists have dug a network of **tunnels** under the site, and two are open to the public for an extra $12. Everybody talks about them, but most visitors find them only slightly interesting.

Late morning is when the main site begins to get crowded with day trippers, so leave it to them for a while, and head a couple of kilometers down the road to **Las Sepulturas Archaeological Site**. The main site of Copán was a government and ceremonial center, but Las Sepulturas was where the local upper class lived. It's one of the few Mayan residential areas that have been found, and provides a fascinating look at the everyday life of the people.

After an hour or so at Las Sepulturas, it's time to think

about lunch. You could take a short taxi ride back to the town of Copán Ruinas, and eat in a nice restaurant, but you still have a lot to see today, so it might be better just to brave the tourist hordes and have an overpriced and generic (but quick) lunch at the cafeteria at the park.

After lunch, visit the **Museum of Mayan Sculpture**, adjacent to the ruins. The museum costs an extra five bucks, but it's well worth it. Many of the original art treasures of Copán are displayed here in the museum, protected from the elements, while the *in situ* versions are actually clever replicas.

The centerpiece of the museum is a life-sized reproduction of the Rosalila Temple, in all its original pink splen-

ALTERNATE PLAN

If you're **traveling with kids**, you may find that their interest in the ancient Maya is limited. Smaller children may not be up for long hikes. Take them to the **kids' museum** in Copán Ruinas (see below), then divide your day between **Macaw Mountain** and the **hot springs**.

🚶 dor. The weathered gray stones that we see at Mayan sites today are in fact only shadows of their original beauty, when they were painted in bright colors.

Here you'll find the finest collection of Mayan sculpture in the world, over 3,000 pieces, many of them mounted in the facades of six reconstructed buildings. Highlights include four of the most beautiful stelae from the site, the original facade of the Ball Court, and the original Altar Q, with its relief depicting the 16 kings of Copán.

By the time you've explored the museum, it will be late in the afternoon, and the day-tripping hordes will be thinning out, but you still have time for another stroll through the ruins. I think you'll find it quite interesting to take a second look after you've seen the museum and learned a bit about the history of the city. Entry to the park is $10, which also includes the Sepulturas archaeological site. Entry to the Museum of Mayan Sculpture is $5. The park and the Sculpture Museum are open daily 8am-4pm. The **Copán Guide Association** offers tours of the Copán Ruins, starting at $20. You can arrange a tour on the spot at the park entrance, but it's wiser to reserve ahead. *Info: Tel. 504-651-4018.*

You've spent a long day soaking up culture, and done a lot of walking, so in the evening reward yourselves with a cold drink and a nice dinner in **Copán Ruinas**, a charming colonial village of cobblestone streets and adobe buildings with cheerful tile roofs.

The **Tunkul Restaurant and Bar** is one of the main hangouts in town. The owners are friendly locals who also run tours in the area. It's a capital place to get the latest local gossip, and compare notes with other hip travelers (the square tourists rushed through the ruins, then blew out of town this afternoon, without even noticing the quaint village, much less stopping for a beer and a chat with the locals).

Sunday
Rise and shine! This morning, you're going to hike through some of the most beautiful countryside in Honduras, up to **Los Sapos**, a minor Mayan

SIGHTS

site on a hill overlooking the valley of Copán. The carvings are pretty worn down, and aren't terribly interesting, but the view up here is splendid, and it's a good excuse for a moderate hike through the forest. Los Sapos is on the grounds of a very nice resort hotel called **Hacienda San Lucas**. You could also get here by taxi or on horseback.

You can also visit a couple of the **Mayan stelae** that are scattered around the valley. There are at least a half-dozen individual stelae in the area, similar to the ones you saw yesterday in the Great Plaza. The best-known is called **La Pintada**, because it still bears traces of the original red paint. It's higher up the mountain from Los Sapos and has spectacular views.

Just before lunchtime, head for the **Macaw Mountain Bird Park**, one of the area's most popular attractions. Scarlet macaws, parrots and toucans in a rainbow of colors flit about in large walk-in aviaries. The park is also a working coffee plantation, and you may spot many species of wild birds.

They have a nice little river-side café here, where you can have lunch and a cup of world-class coffee from their high-altitude coffee farm, **Finca Miramundo**. There's lots to see here (kids will especially like it), so make an afternoon of it.

Info: www.macawmountain.com; Tel. 504-651-4245. Open daily 9am-5pm. Entry $10.

After a long day of walking through the forests, a nice soak in hot water is just what the doctor ordered. By the time you've been in Copán Ruinas ten minutes, you'll have heard about **Agua Caliente**, the local *balneario* or hot springs – every other person in town seems to be offering to take you there. The hot water from the springs mixes with the cool river water, and there are two pools where you can soak your tired joints, while enjoying the lovely green surroundings.

Info: Open daily 8am-8pm. Entrance fee about $3.

Copán Ruinas
Many of the thousands who visit the archaeological park each year zip in and out without even stopping in the

nearby town. They're missing a real treat. **Copán Ruinas** is a charming colonial village of cobblestone streets and adobe buildings with cheerful tile roofs.

As the center of tourism in the area, Copán Ruinas has a good selection of hotels and restaurants, and plenty of facilities for travelers, including three banks and several internet cafés. Although it's usually bustling with tourists, most of them are fairly hip tourists, here to enjoy the local ambience for a few days – most of the t-shirt-and-ice-cream-cone crowd make a day trip to the ruins, then rush to Roatan.

A couple of small museums on the main square are each worth a quick visit. The **Maya Archaeology Museum** has a collection of artifacts from the Copán site, including some nice ceramic and jade artworks.

Info: Open Mon-Sat 8am-noon and 1-4pm. Entry about $2.

A new museum called **Casa K'inich** (House of the Sun) is aimed at children, with a variety of interactive exhibits about the ancient Maya. Local teachers guide kids through some fun activities – they'll learn not only about the history of the Maya, but a little about languages as well, as all the signs are in English, Spanish and Chortí Maya.

Info: Open Mon-Sat 8am-noon and 1-5pm. Free.

There is a new airfield just inside the border with Guatemala. You can fly from Guatemala City with **Jungle Flying**. This new service makes day trips from Guatemala City possible. Flights onward to Roatan are also available.

Info: Tel 2360-4917.

Hedman Alas runs first-class air-conditioned **buses** three times a day from/to San Pedro Sula, with connections to Tegucigalpa and La Ceiba.

BEST SLEEPS & EATS

Copán sees travelers of every class, from upscale ecotourists to the backpacker crowd, so there's a wide range of lodging choices. At the bus station, you'll be mobbed by hustlers offering to find you cheap hotel rooms and/or local tours.

Hotel Marina Copán $$$$
This peaceful oasis is located right on the Central Park. Guests rave about the professional and personal service. The oldest hotel in town, it's a major part of local history. When archaeologists and researchers began coming to Copán in the early 1900s,

many of them stayed at the home of the Welchez family, which built the hotel in 1945.

The architecture is classic colonial style, with lots of lovely tile and carved wood furnishings. The 50 rooms and suites are spacious and spotless, with tile floors and nice art on the walls. All have private bath, AC, ceiling fans, TV and phone. The most picturesque rooms are in the older rear section. The pool is something special, lovely tile surrounded by tropical greenery. There's a spa and a sauna, a gift shop, free parking in a secure lot and free wireless internet.

Glifos Restaurant is generally considered one of Copán's finest – it's a little pricey, but you won't be disappointed. The poolside Jaguar Venado Bar has live music on weekend nights. Enjoy a cup of the rich local coffee and a *tres leches* cake at the Café Welchez. *Info: www.hotelmarinacopan.com; Tel. 504-651-4070, 504-651-4071 or 800-893-9131 US.*

Posada Real de Copán $$$$
If you'd rather stay just out of town at a place with a grand view, this is a good choice. Just a few minutes from town and from the

ruins, the Posada Real sits on a hilltop with a panoramic view of the Copán valley. The 80 rooms are quite spacious, with tile floors, pastel walls, modern bathrooms, AC, direct phones and cable TV. There's a pool and Jacuzzi, a gift shop, plenty of parking, and a hiking trail. The restaurant and bar are elegant, but the food is good, not great. *Info: www.posadarealdecopan.com; Tel. 504-651-4480, 504-651-4481 or 504-651-4482.*

Hacienda San Lucas $$$$
This is a very special place: not just a lovely country inn with wonderful views of the Copán Valley, not just one of the most character-filled places to stay in the entire country, but a heart-warming story of sustainable tourism.

The old *hacienda* (farmhouse) has been in the Cueva family for 100 years. It's located on 300 acres of forested grounds, directly overlooking the ruins. In fact, a smaller archaeological site called Los Sapos is located here on the grounds.

In 2000, Flavia Cueva, a local Honduran lady who lived in the US for several years, converted the property to an ecolodge. Now, a lot of folks in Honduras call their places ecolodges, but Ms Cueva really did things right. She restored the hacienda in classic style, and the contractors used only local materials and local craftsmen. In fact, they used no power tools or modern machinery at all.

The inn, originally just two rooms, was a huge success, and it has since become a favorite of chic ecotourists, and has been written up in all sorts of high-tone travel magazines. Six new rooms were added in 2005.

You'll find no AC, phones or TVs here, nor will you miss them.

SLEEPS & EATS

There is electricity, but it's provided by a small solar-power installation, so after dark most of the light is provided by candles, which many guests find to be a wonderful part of the atmosphere. The rooms are pure rustic charm, but they are no funky shacks. The bathrooms are nice and modern, with plenty of hot water, and the beds are comfortable. Fine woodwork and local art grace the walls.

The cuisine is likewise earthy and local. Homemade tortillas and tamales and fresh vegetables from the farm anchor the menu. There's plenty of good hiking and horseback riding to be done around here, and plenty of hammocks in which to recover from same. And the final clincher? There are a couple of friendly Labradors! *Info: www.haciendasanlucas.com; Tel. 504-651-4495.*

La Casa de Café $$$
This cozy bed and breakfast is four blocks from the Central Park. It's been drawing rave reviews for the fine service and home-like atmosphere.

The 10 rooms each have private bath and ceiling fan ($45 double). The common area has cable TV and a wide selection of books and videos about the Mayan ruins and other local attractions. There's a pretty garden with hammocks, and an impressive view of the valley and the mountains.

True to its name, the House of Coffee serves a damn fine cup of estate coffee from local growers. Breakfasts are hot and hearty, with ham and eggs and fresh tortillas. *Info: www.casadecafecopan.com; Tel. 504-651-4620.*

There are several more moderately-priced hotels in the center of town. Also on the Central Park are **Hotel Los Jaguares** (*Tel. 504-651-4451*), which has 10 rooms with private bath and AC; and **Hotel Yaragua** (*Tel. 504-651-4147; www.yaragua.com*), home base for **Yaragua Tours**, which runs adventure and cultural tours in the region.

Copán has several cheap dormitory-style lodgings, a couple of which are famous stops on the backpacker circuit. **Hotel Los Gemelos** (*Tel. 504-651-4077*), a couple blocks from the Central Park, has small but clean rooms for under $10, plus an internet café.

The humble but friendly **Via Via** (*Tel. 504-651-4652; Email copan.honduras@viaviacafe.com*) has dorm beds and rooms with private bath. The restaurant has some vegetarian dishes. Another good backpacker option is **Iguana Azul**, three blocks from the center (*Tel. 504-651-4620; Email casadecafe@mayanet.hn*).

Twisted Tanya's $$
This famous local spot is a good restaurant and a lively bar. On a second-floor terrace with a view of the mountains, a mix of tourists, expats and locals eats, drinks and gets twisted. The

DINING OUT IN COPÁN RUINAS

As one of the top tourist draws in Honduras, the Copán area has a wide selection of restaurants. Thanks to the rich ecotourists and the poor backpackers (who have more in common than you might think), you'll find more healthy and creative dining options here than some other places in the country. However, you can also find plenty of overpriced tourist chow, and not only at the cafeteria at the ruins site.

Several of the hotels have good restaurants, notably the upscale cuisine of **Glifos** at the Marina Copán and the roll-your-own-tamales candlelight dinners at **Hacienda San Lucas**.

Inexpensive and lively restaurants form a cluster for a block or two around the Central Park. If you stroll around here, you won't fail to find a spot for dinner.

The nightlife scene is fairly low-key – there are plenty of places for a friendly drink, but no hopping discos.

There are several little spots around town that serve up fresh fruit smoothies (*licuados*), a cool and delicious treat any time of day.

vivacious Tanya is a great source of information on travels in the area, as well as the North Coast and Bay Islands.

The ever-changing menu includes an international variety of beef, chicken, seafood, pasta and vegetarian dishes, with an emphasis on fresh local ingredients and a dash of Bay Islands style. "If it's in the market, it's on the menu."

How about conch soup, an avocado shrimp cocktail, or seafood pasta? Healthy bites include grilled portobello mushrooms, vegetarian curry and homemade hummus. Meat lovers won't be complaining once they get a load of the huge filet mignons and ribeyes. The happy hour (4-6pm) is famous, with Tanya and Nelly whipping up any fancy cocktail you can imagine from nice fresh ingredients, and a variety of hip music on the stereo. *Info: www.twistedtanya.com; Tel. 504-651-4182. Closed Sunday.*

Llama del Bosque $$

This local classic has been around since 1975, serving up *comida típica* such as *baleadas, parrilladas* and *anafre de chorizo*, as well as tourist fare like sandwiches, salads and spaghetti. Most dishes are less than $5. The restaurant is not named for a South American animal, but rather for a common tree in the region that sports flame-colored flowers. *Info: Tel. 504-651-4431. Open daily for breakfast, lunch and dinner.*

COFFEE

The area around Copán is **coffee-growing country**. Most restaurants are proud of their fresh-roasted brew. I highly recommend a visit to the local coffee plantations. This web page has a lot of information about Honduran coffee: www.sweetmarias.com/coffee.central.honduras.html.

Tunkul Restaurant and Bar $$

A block from the Central Park, this local institution is *the* place to meet the local posse and hear all the latest news about the area. Owner Mike is a local who lived in the States for a few years, and he'll make you feel at home. The food is a mix of Central American cuisine (*baleadas* and *quesadillas* made with home-made tortillas, *anafres* and the infamous *Nachos Catrachos*) and international bar food (cheeseburgers, chicken wings, pasta and salads). Steaks, *pinchos* and chicken dishes are grilling over a wood fire. Portions are large, and most dishes are under $6.

Happy hour begins here just as it ends over at Tanya's. Draft beer, a decent selection of wine and a full liquor bar keep the multilingual conversation going. Occasionally there's a bit of live music. El Tunkul is home base for **Go Native Tours**, which runs tours all over the region. *Info: Tel. 504-651-4410.*

Carnitas Nía Lola $$$
This is another popular spot in town, a wild-looking building with splendid views of the valley from the second floor. It's famous for huge portions of grilled meats, including the namesake *carnitas* (hunks of grilled pork), *alambritos* (chopped steak with bacon, onions, cheese and peppers) and *pinchos* (skewers with huge hunks of beef, pork, chicken and vegetables). Also tacos, *anafre* and other local favorites. Happy hour here is also lively. *Info: Tel. 504-651-4196. Open daily 7am-10pm.*

La Casa de Maíz $$
This place celebrates the humble Honduran staple, corn (or maize, as our British cousins call it). *Tamales*, corn flour wrapped in a corn husk and filled with meat or beans, don't get any more authentic than this. If you're feeling corny, try one of the less-familiar items such as *pupusas*, *montucas*, *ticucos*, *atoles* or *chilates*. A pleasant outdoor terrace a block from the Central Park. *Info: Tel. 504-651-4080. Open daily 7am-9pm.*

Coffee Casita $$
If you love coffee, have lunch at the Macaw Mountain Bird Park (a don't-miss attraction in its own right – see earlier in this chapter). Their shade-grown estate coffee comes from their high-altitude plantation up at Finca Miramundo, is roasted right here in a quaint old Turkish roaster, and brewed up on a modern Swiss machine. Damn good cup! Damn good cup!

Enjoy your cappuccino or espresso with a nice lunch at this beautiful outdoor café, overlooking a rushing mountain stream and surrounded by tropical verdure and resplendent birds. FYI, both photos below were taken at Macaw Mountain Bird Park. *Info: www.macawmountain.com; Tel. 504-651-4245. Open daily 9am-5pm.*

9. THE PACIFIC COAST

HIGHLIGHTS

▲ Sailfish – anglers from around the world come for 10 to 20 daily hookups

▲ Vegging Out – or just hanging out on the beach or by your hotel's pool

▲ Bird Watching – last one to see a resplendent quetzal buys the drinks!

COORDINATES

Guatemala's Pacific coast stretches for more than 150 miles – almost all of it deserted dark sand beaches. There is a short road running just up the coast between Puerto San José and Monterico. This area is frequented by international and Guatemalan beach lovers. A few other roads run from the main highway, ending in small fishing towns.

INTRO

The Pacific coast of Guatemala boasts wonderful, untamed, **black sand beaches**. The surf is wild and the sand steep. These are beautiful beaches but a little on the dangerous side for swimming. Sailfish and tuna are available in huge numbers offshore. Most of the nicest lodgings along the coast are dedicated fishing lodges, which are world famous for being the most productive sailfish fisheries in the world.

The area is popular with well-off Guatemalan families enjoying a weekend at the sea and with gringo anglers hoping to catch and release a couple of dozen sailfish.

There are a few wonderful lodges quite well set up for doing nothing more than hanging around in hammocks.

SIGHTS

A PACIFIC COAST WEEKEND

The plan for the weekend includes hammocks, sun and surf combined with fresh fish, fruity tropical cocktails and plenty of time in or near the swimming pool.

Friday Evening
Drive down as early as possible and check into one of the lovely lodges like **Isleta Gaia** or **Cayman Suites**. Both are right on the beach and have great bars/restaurants.

Gaia is isolated, hard to get to and very tranquil. Cayman Suites is just off the main road, has most resort amenities and is popular with Guatemalans down from the city for a long weekend with the kids and family. Have a nice dinner; dip into the pool and down a couple of *tragos* of rum. Listen to the surf. Go to bed early—there's not much else to do anyway.

Saturday

Wake early and take a long walk along the beach, looking for interesting things that have washed up overnight. You can do as the locals do, and look for the tractor-like marks in the sand that mean a turtle has come ashore to nest. Actually, it's best if you don't find any, as the locals would almost certainly have beat you to it and all you will see is a messy hole where the fresh-laid eggs *used* to be.

The drive along the coast is disappointing. You can't really see much. I suggest you spend your Pacific Coast weekend enjoying the beach and your hotel facilities rather than driving around sightseeing. There is just not that much to see. The pot-hole-strewn road along the coast runs about a half-mile inland and offers few, if any, glimpses of the sea. The road is lined with shacks, crummy-looking stores and third-world squalor. Drive slowly so you don't run over any pigs. You have to look for small sand roads off the main highway leading to the beach to see the stunning black sand and huge waves.

GETTING NAKED

It is not okay to go around naked on the beaches here. Guatemalans are generally a conservative lot and dress well at all times – even at the beach. Most hotels will not tolerate nudity in and around their pools. So, no topless sunbathing, and leave the thong in your suitcase unless everyone else at your hotel is letting their stuff hang out.

Here and there you will see small **loofah** farms along the roadside. You can see the green ones still growing on the trellised vines. White ones, dried in the sun, can be bought from roadside stands for under $1.

ALTERNATE PLAN

Check into **Pacific Fins** for an all-inclusive weekend of fishing for sailfish, tuna, wahoo and **dorado**. Throw the sailfish back to be caught again and keep the tuna and dorado for dinner.

With luck, they will have local fresh snook (*robalo* in Spanish) on the menu for dinner. This is one of my favorite local fish and is not to be missed.

SIGHTS

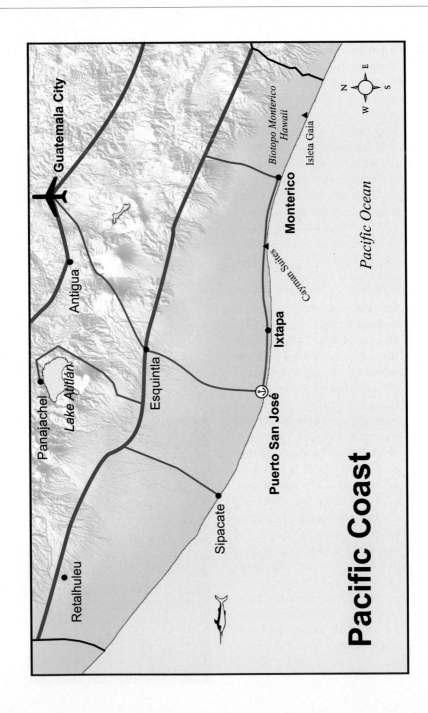

SIGHTS

Sunday
A beach weekend is just that—time on the beach—so wake up at a reasonable hour, have coffee and other morning sustenance and then take another long beachside walk. Cool off in the pool. Pack up your now-sandy belongings, put lotion on your sunburn and head back.

A WEEK ON THE PACIFIC COAST

Even though some could spend an entire week soaking up sandy activities on the beach, there are more sailfish off the coast of Guatemala than you can shake a stick at. So go shake that stick and go fly fishing. You can still find plenty of time for the beach. Check into one of Guatemala's top fishing lodges like Pacific Fins or Sailfish Bay. Sailfish, wahoo and tuna are reliable catches. Spend two or three days fishing and another couple of days doing beach things.

The Pacific coast offers absolutely the best sailfishing in the world. Beaches are mostly dark, steep and wild. There are a couple of smallish eco preserves. Towns along the coast are mostly run-down, and the limited coastal road gives tourists a great view of third world squalor but little view of the beautiful coastline. Activity choices are simple: fishing for sailfish or lounging around on the beach. Shopping for items of interests to tourists is pretty much non-existent. There are some eco-tours you can take through the **Biotopo-Monterico Hawaii**.

Sailfish are the number one reason North Americans come to the Pacific coast of Guatemala. This is the **sailfish capital of the world**. Catch and release of over 30 sails per day per boat is not unusual. Several lodges cater to anglers.

Monterico
Monterico used to be one of the top Pacific destinations for vacationers from Guatemala City. While it still bustles on the weekends, the town is more an average, not-particularly-interesting run-down Central American town with *waaay* too much traffic. There are a few **fading-glory hotels**

and a dirty beach, but I suspect that most tourists will prefer staying in one of the nicer, newer hotels outside town.

Monterico has become known for **Centro de Estudios Conservacionistas'** work accepting turtle eggs from locals and hatching them in their facilities for controlled release on the beaches in and near town. In spite of what tourist agencies may tell you, very few turtles actually come ashore here anymore. In 2008, only four leatherbacks are known to have come ashore, and only one of those actually managed to lay eggs that were not snatched by the local egg hunters, *hueveros*.

Many locals have never heard of this program or ignore it, and keep all the eggs they find to sell as a local alternative to Viagra. Beaches up and down the coast are patrolled day and night by locals in ATVs looking for turtles coming ashore to nest. They rob the nests to sell the eggs and pay no attention as feral dogs harass the turtles as they try to return through the surf.

Ixtapa

Kind of a stinky port town, Ixtapa has little to offer. However, just outside town, the wonderful **Pacific Fins fishing lodge** is probably the nicest place to stay on the coast. Their rooms and food are aimed at satisfying well-off North American anglers who spend as much as four thousand dollars for a week of fishing and indulging in steaks, lobster, giant hamburgers, hundreds of beers and lots of mojitos. The fishing is tops and the anglers all seem to love the pampering.

Unlike many fishing lodges, activities for the ladies have been taken into account. Spa and beauty treatments are available, and excursions to nearby Antigua for a wide variety of activities (art gallery visits, wildlife hikes, volcano climbs) can be arranged easily.

Isleta Gaia

Named for the mother of Zeus, Gaia is a simple, uncomplicated beachside resort. Actually, to call it a "resort" might be stretching things some. They have a nice pool and a large palapa with restaurant and bar.

It is located on a small barrier island, right on the beach at the edge of the sand. The breeze blows through, the sound of the surf hypnotizes. The delights of the restaurant and bar (French chef) mean you will need plenty of hammock time to sleep off your meals. There is not much else to do anyway other than take long walks on the beach, read and watch the birds. Some guests end up staying for months.

If you are a real birder, this would be a great spot to come for seabirds and a couple of

SAND FLEAS

Many Guatemalan beaches are thick with irritating **sand fleas**, almost invisible little buggers that swarm around the beach. Many people have their favorite sauces to drive away the little ankle-biters but, to my knowledge, none of these spreads works for everyone. Many swear by **Avon's Skin-So-Soft**, so it's a good idea to bring some as well as the usual high-DEET mosquito repellent.

exotic endemics that live nearby. You can do it on your own or arrange in advance with **Cayaya Birding** for a whole package. Boats from the lodge can take you for miles in the lagoon looking for zone-tailed hawks, social flycatchers or Wilson's warbler.

SIGHTS

SLEEPS & EATS

BEST SLEEPS & EATS

There are relatively few nice hotels in the Pacific area and no upscale resorts.

BEST OF THE BEST ON THE PACIFIC COAST
Hotel Isleta de Gaia $$$

Gaia, named for the mother of Zeus, is a simple, uncomplicated beachside resort. Actually, to call it a "resort" might be stretching things some. They have a nice pool and a large

palapa with restaurant and bar. Kayaks pretty much round out the amenities. I don't see the lack of big-resort services as a problem, quite the opposite. The best thing about Gaia is the location: right at the top of the beach slope. The surf is only feet from your door. The sound of the surf lulls you into a morphine-like state of torpor. After a couple of hours in your hammock, you just can't imagine leaving or even moving very much.

There is no crowd here. There is nothing to do but take a walk on the beach or lounge around. If you open the blinds on your bungalow, the warm trade winds just blow through. It's not at all fancy, but is so peaceful and refreshing that it attracts an upscale crowd from Guatemala City as well as the American ambassador, the President of Guatemala, writers, artists and others looking for a serene atmosphere to recharge their batteries. Some guests end up staying for months. Don't come here for action. Come here to take long afternoon naps. *Info: Near Las Lisas. www.isleta-de-gaia.com; Tel. 502-7885-0044.*

Cayman Suites $$$

All by itself, right on the beach, the Cayman Suites is a newish hotel popular with Guatemalan families. The rooms are very comfortable, with air-conditioning, cable TV, small refrigerators and upscale bathroom fixtures (no internet). There are all sorts of things to appeal to kids: playground equipment, a small soccer field, a great pool with kiddy area and swim-up bar and a pirate tower. The beach location is killer but the place is fairly sterile. If you just want to veg out by the sea and don't mind a few kids running around, Cayman Suites will work just fine. Adults and kids spend hours cutting donuts on the beach right in front of the hotel on four wheelers while talking on their cell phones.

The restaurant is right at the edge of the sand under a huge, marvelous palapa. The food is ordinary but be sure to try the local specialties: *robalo* (snook) and local shrimp. *Info: Kilometer 10.5 between Iztapa and Monterico. www.caymansuites.com.gt; Tel. 502-2332-7161.*

Sailfish Bay Lodge $$$

One of the top three or four fishing lodges in the country, Sailfish Bay is well known for comfortable, top-quality facilities and simply the best sail fishing in the world. Their repeat visitor rate is over 80%. Unlike the other lodges, they are right on the beach and have great views.

They have nine well-equipped boats using mostly Penn and Shimano tackle, and focus particularly on fly fishing. *Info: Iztapa. www.sailfishbay.com; Tel. 502-5744-2562, 800-638-7405 US.*

Pacific Fins $$$$

This is the top fishing lodge in the country, with numerous catch and release records. It is a very comfortable and professional fishing lodge. Managers Scott and Natalie keep things running nicely. The lodge appeals primarily to North American anglers looking to hook up. Anglers have discovered that sailfish swarm offshore in world-class numbers. Their two-bedroom villas are large, air conditioned and fully appointed. There are two bars, and the restaurant serves excellent gringo-style food, focusing on seafood, pasta and steaks. Most of their captains are American and mates speak basic English. Boats and equipment are top notch. You can troll with the latest lures, pitch live bait or fly fish. They usually run about 7 boats, from 31 Bertrams to a Topaz 50, and can fish up to 20 people.

Unlike at many fishing lodges, activities for the ladies have been taken into account. Spa and beauty treatments are available and excursions to nearby Antigua for a wide variety of activities (art gallery visits, wildlife hikes, volcano climbs) can be arranged easily.

Food, lodging and fishing are all-inclusive. Only alcohol is an extra charge. The facility is surrounded by high walls and, for most tourists, there is little of interest within walking distance except for the wonderful bar/restaurant El Capitán, which is almost next door. *Info: Near Iztapa. www.pacificfins.com; Tel. 502-5205-1010, 888-700-3467, 888-700- 3467 US.*

Casa Vieja Lodge $$$

Another top lodge for sailfish, Casa Vieja has recently updated their US-style lodgings, and now has 16 well-appointed rooms.

Formerly Fins 'N' Feathers, the boats, captains and equipment are considered to be some of the best in Guatemala. The spectacular palapa-covered bar and restaurant is a great place to relax after a long day spent fishing. A great deal of money and effort has been invested.

Their six boats run from a 37 Gamefisherman to a Merritt 43. High-speed Shimanos are spooled with 20lb but all boats have a rigged 80lb rig ready to pitch to the occasional "beast." Fly fishermen are accommodated. The lodge is surrounded by high walls and is located in the shabby town of Puerto San José. The usual excursions to Antigua can be arranged but there is not much of interest for tourists in the immediate area. *Info: Puerto San José. www.casaviejalodge.com; Tel. 502-5228-9916, 866-846-9121 US.*

El Capitán $$

This is the place to gorge on ceviche and other seafood dishes. Whole snapper (*pargo entero*) is not to be missed. This is a funky waterfront bar/restaurant with loads of character. It is usually jammed with Guatemalans visiting from the city. Salsa music blares and the sexy waitresses sashay through the tables, bringing cold, cold beer and wonderful ceviche. This my favorite place to eat on the Pacific coast. It is very hard to find, since you have to thread your way through several extremely funky local streets dodging pigs and chickens to get here. Locals will give you all sorts of conflicting directions, but asking is really the only way to find it. It is in a small village about half way between Puerto

SLIM PICKINS'

There are few restaurants of note in the area. Some of the upscale hotels have passable restaurants, justifying their high prices with spectacular views. For the most part the food is unremarkable. The best thing to do is to **focus on local fish and shrimp**. Ceviche can be wonderful here. Tilapia is farm raised in the area, and you are likely to be underhandedly fed this mushy and insipid fish in place of the more interesting varieties listed on menus. This is exactly what happens in many US restaurants as well. Shrimp is caught offshore and raised locally in ponds. If the shrimp are huge, they are probably farm raised.

San José and Iztapa. After you turn off the main road, go straight ahead until you have to turn. Go right for about a half mile until you see the sign. *Info: Iztapa.*

BEST SPORTS & RECREATION

Fishing

The Pacific coast offers absolutely **the best sailfishing in the world**. Beaches are mostly dark, steep and wild. There are a couple of smallish eco-preserves. Towns along the coast are mostly run-down, and the limited coastal road gives tourists a great view of them but little view of the beautiful coastline. Activity choices are simple: fishing for sailfish or lounging around on the beach. Shopping for items of interests to tourists is pretty much non-existent. There are some eco-tours you can take through the Biotopo-Monterico Hawaii.

Sailfish are the number one reason North Americans come to the Pacific coast of Guatemala. This is the sailfish capital of the world. Catch and release of over 30 sails per day per boat is not unusual. Several lodges cater to this.

By law, all sailfish must be

> ### MORE SLIM PICKINS' ...
>
> Forget about shopping in the Pacific area. A few of the fishing lodges sell shirts, hats and sunglasses in their gift shops but that's about it. You can buy loofahs from stalls along the road in some areas.
>
> **Forget about nightlife** too, at least any that would appeal to most tourists. Stay in your lodge at night drinking rum around the pool or go to bed early. Local bars are generally to be avoided.

released. This does not stop the offshore commercial fishing long liners from scooping them up by the thousands, along with dorado and tuna, and transshipping them through other countries to be consumed mostly in the US, often identified as tuna or swordfish.

Most of the sport fishing is

done rather far offshore. About 30 miles out, there is a steep drop-off that causes an up-welling of deep currents that attracts huge swarms of small bait fish. These small fish at-tract medium size predators like small tuna, dorado, blue runners and such. These guys, weighing anywhere from a couple of pounds to about 20 pounds, attract sailfish, wa-hoo, larger tuna and marlin. These attract anglers from all over the world.

CIRCLE HOOKS

Circle hooks work great! Hookup ratios are high and, once hooked, it's hard for a fish to throw a circle hook. The best part is that they are quite easy to remove for a quick release once the fish has been brought into the boat.

SPORTS & RECREATION

SPORTS & RECREATION

Saving the Turtles?

Organizations in Monterico are known for their work accepting turtle eggs from locals and hatching them in their facilities for controlled release on the beaches in and near town. Locals are supposed to hand over 50% of their egg finds in return for being able to keep the rest. Sounds good.

Many locals have never heard of this program, or ignore it and keep all the eggs they find to sell as a local alternative to Viagra. Beaches up and down the coast are patrolled day and night by locals in ATVs looking for turtles coming ashore to nest. They rob the nests to sell the eggs and pay no attention as feral dogs harass the turtles as they try to return through the surf.

Hotel owners and tourism officials extol the wonders of the huge *arribadas* of **olive Ridley and leatherback turtles** that supposedly come ashore in the thousands during August and September. They are dreaming of a not-so-distant past. Few turtles come ashore anymore and of those that do, very, very few make it past the human and canine predators who await them.

TURTLE WORSHIP

Observing turtles as they come onto the beach at night to lay eggs is a possible activity but, even though it is prohibited by law to collect the eggs or disturb the turtles, you may have to argue with locals who patrol the beaches at night in their ATVs looking for nests to rob. **Turtle eggs are reputed to make men more macho** – rivaling Viagra. Young, local macho-types eat them while drinking beer in run-down cantinas hoping for good luck and vigor later in the evening. Sad but true.

Well-intentioned organizations raise babies from hatchlings and release them for the delight of tourists after they hatch. This raises questions about the best places for releases so returning mothers will have the best chance to escape the clutches of hungry Guatemalan peasants and feral dogs. Lights on the beach are well known to put off returning mother turtles.

The tourist who places their bet on the first baby to reach the sea wins a free dinner at any of the hotels in town. Fun? Yes. Does it raise money for the study of turtles? Yes, but probably not much. None of the hotels offer a decent dinner anyway.

Few turtles are seen in the area anymore. You are much more likely to see turtle carcasses being devoured by wild beach dogs than the successful nesting and return to the sea of these amazing creatures.

Of course the solution is to ban all harvesting of turtle eggs and set aside hundreds of miles of protected and patrolled coastline, allowing turtles to nest naturally. Get your checkbook ready.

SPORTS & RECREATION

10. THE CARIBBEAN COAST

HIGHLIGHTS
▲ Visit the Garífuna community

▲ Uncrowded beaches of wildlife refuge Punta de Manabique

▲ Río Dulce Canyon

▲ Biotopo Chocón Machacas

COORDINATES

Livingston and **Río Dulce** are the only salubrious towns in Guatemala's Caribbean coastal area. Río Dulce is easily reached by road or boat from Livingston. Livingston itself is on an island and is only reachable by launch.

INTRO

Guatemala's Caribbean coast, with remnants of Garífuna and Mayan cultures and a fondness for reggae and spicy fish stews, attracts an international crowd of hip travelers. The weather is warm year round and the sea is calm. In **Livingston**, life is slow: dogs sleep soundly in the middle of the street, and local Rastafarians puff ganja and bop to sounds only they can hear. Yachts from all over the world congregate in **Río Dulce's** inland, fresh-water harbor. The remote and seldom-visited beaches of wildlife refuge **Punta de Manabique** beckon the adventurous traveler.

A RÍO DULCE WEEKEND

Río Dulce means "Sweet River." It begins in Lago Isabal, the largest lake in Guatemala, and ends at the Caribbean Sea. Yachtsmen from around the world congregate here to take advantage of the inland harbor. Bird watchers and manatee worshippers will find plenty to do.

Río Dulce is a grimy crossroads town characterized by the usual small shops, grubby cafés and whorehouses catering to passing truck drivers. Its claims to fame include the high bridge that affords a view of the river, the lake itself (a nice lake) and the large community of North American and European yachties who gather there because of the deep water, protected anchorage and low cost of living.

Most lodging in the area is of the budget and backpacker type. There is no reason to linger here other than to catch a boat down the river, or for a cruise on the lake.

If you are traveling through Río Dulce on your way to or from Tikal and need a place to stay overnight, I suggest you skip Río Dulce the town for an overnight stay and try the **Hotel Ecológico Finca Ixobel** further on up the road towards Tikal south of Poptún.

SIGHTS

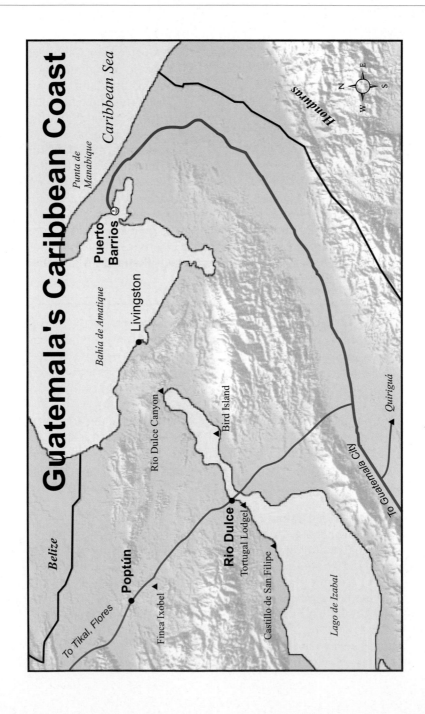

The Río Dulce area is commonly touted as one of Guatemala's major tourist attractions, but I can't understand why. The famous cliffs (graffiti-covered) and canyons on the river are pretty, but mostly underwhelming. The **hot springs** and **waterfall** are well worth a miss. If you want to trim your over-ambitious Guatemala itinerary, you shouldn't feel too bad about skipping the Río Dulce area.

There is no industry along the river and no roads: therefore, there's little pollution. This also means that all transport is aquatic. Popular activities in the area are **hiking, bird watching, sailing, fishing** and **kayaking**.

The usual way to get to Río Dulce is by express bus from Guatemala City. You can also arrive by boat from Livingston. The ride along the river is one of the main reasons people visit the area.

Friday
If you arrive in Río Dulce by road, you'll need to slog your luggage a little way through town to the dock under the bridge to transfer by boat to **Tortugal Lodge**.

I suggest relaxing in the lodge for whatever remains of the afternoon, and trying some snook for dinner in the restaurant. This is not an area with wild nightlife, so have another beer in the bar, swap some more travel stories with your new travel pals and go to bed early.

Saturday
Río Dulce highlights include the mildly interesting old Spanish fortress **Castillo de San Felipe** (*photo below*), **Bird Island**, and **Biotopo Chocón Machacas** manatee reserve. The **Río Dulce Canyon** has lofty walls of limestone draped with jungle flora and fauna, and is worth a look.

SIGHTS

All of these sights require a boat. You can arrange a *lancha* and guide for the day at your hotel. If you are traveling on to Livingston, you can see much of this on the two-hour boat trip when you go—no need for a special tour unless you want to take your time birding.

Castillo de San Felipe is an old Spanish fort on the Río Dulce, near the top of Lake Izabel, built in the 1600s to fight the burgeoning pirate trade. The fort has a crummy restaurant and a decent swimming area. Personally, I would not pay anything extra to take in its charms.

Bird Island is a small island downstream from Río Dulce, infested with cormorants (diving ducks), egrets, and other water birds. Twitchers will love it.

The small **Biotopo Chocón Machacas** is an area of mangrove-lined lagoons connected by small rivers, which can be explored for hours. It is home to approximately 200 species of birds and over 50 different species of trees. It was created to protect manatees, and you may see some as they lazily forage. Wandering around here is probably the best of all the activities in the area and gets my vote for a full afternoon of leisurely wildlife watching.

Sunday
The best thing to do is to combine your departure from Río Dulce with another boat ride along the river through the picturesque canyons to **Livingston**. Your hotel can arrange the regular boat to stop for you or, for a little more money, you can hire a private boat to take you more slowly through the river valley that leads to Livingston

and the Caribbean. It's a nice ride, and takes a couple of hours depending on the number of stops and side trips you make.

A WEEKEND IN LIVINGSTON

Livingston seems almost undiscovered. Dogs sleep soundly in the middle of the street and the locals seem to have the place all to themselves. There are a couple of interesting restaurants serving local specialties. It is a good base for exploring the river, or a jumping off point for Belize or Honduras.

Friday
You can get to Livingston from Guatemala City by taking an express bus to **Puerto Barrios** and then transferring to a boat to get to the island town. Puerto Barrios is not a pleasant town, so instead I suggest getting to Livingston by the much more picturesque route via Río Dulce. The nicest way to travel between Río Dulce and Livingston is by boat—it's much prettier and more relaxing.

If you planned well, you should arrive in Livingston in the mid-afternoon by boat, *una lancha* from Río Dulce. "Luxury" express buses should take you to Río Dulce directly from Guatemala City with only one or two stops in about four hours. The boat ride down the river from Río Dulce should take you a couple of hours with plenty of time for stops along the way to admire wildlife or take photographs.

Livingston is a funky but clean river mouth town on an island in the Caribbean at the mouth of the Río Dulce. It is advertised as a good place to experience Caribbean **Garífuna** culture, but the remaining Garífuna or Caribbean culture is vanishing fast.

Get your boat to take you directly to the dock at your hotel, the **Posada Delfín**. This hotel is not just on the waterfront, it is built out over the water, and is in a quiet part of the town. Actually, the whole town is quiet.

Back at the hotel, grab a beer and have a chat with other travelers or with the interest-

SIGHTS

ing and colorful Gustavo Turcios, the hotel owner and head of police for the Livingston area.

Saturday
There is really not much to do other than walk around the small town, check out the tourist stores and see what people get up to. It's a friendly town, and everyone says *"buenos días"* so it's quite pleasant to just stroll around. Check out the spirited *fútbol* games every night by the school.

If you did not arrive via the river, be sure to take a *lancha* up the river to Río Dulce. The jungle falls down towering cliffs as you buzz along looking for crocs, birds, and manatees. It's the prettiest thing around.

Walk all the way down to the beach at the end of the Calle Principal just past **Tilingo**

Lingo, and turn left to get to what remains of the **Garífuna** village. You will probably have already made friends with a local urging you to visit his humble abode. If you are comfortable with this you'll probably be okay following along for an afternoon. Otherwise try to arrange for a simple stroll through the village. I find the locals to be a little puzzling at first but friendly, anxious to meet and hang out with tourists and ready to make a buck, if possible.

Sunday
The skippable **Museo Multicultural de Livingston** near the dock covers local culture and wildlife. It's actually a good place to get a grounding on who the locals are and how they live. **Siete Altares** is a nearby set of waterfalls—quite pleasant. Even though it's close to town, be sure to hire someone from your hotel to go with you for security reasons.

Beaches near town are almost always murky due to the outflow of the river, but there is a reasonably nice beach, **Playa Blanca**, about seven miles outside town. Hire a boat and take lunch. Birding along the way is great.

If you can, go back up the river to Río Dulce on your way back to Guatemala City or wherever is next on your itinerary. Avoid the depressing Puerto Barrios at all costs.

Note: Due to recent security issues (a gringo murder and the kidnapping of some NGO workers), Livingston and Río Dulce are almost empty of tourists lately. This will change. Local authorities have responded to the loss of tourist dollars by implementing extensive security measures in the area and, as a result, there is a good feeling of safety and tranquility. Gustavo Turcios, head of police for the region, told me there are almost no "difficult elements" left and encouraged me to feel free to roam around the town at night visiting bars and clubs until the tiny hours with no worries. I felt fine doing exactly this. He tells me the tame hippie colony is no trouble at all—I got the sense that he doesn't care how much pot they smoke.

Punta de Manabique
Puerto Barrios is a real drag.

SIGHTS

MANGROVES

Mangroves are an amazing family of trees that grow on saltwater shorelines, their roots in the tidal water. A mangrove swamp is a unique ecosystem. The underwater forest of their roots makes a perfect habitat for barnacles, oysters, sponges, and sea squirts, which filter their food from the water as the tide goes in and out. Adolescent **fish** (including snook, snapper, shark, sea trout, tarpon and bonefish), shrimp, lobsters and many other creatures find shelter and food among the mangrove roots. **Birds** and **monkeys** live in the trees. Mangrove wetlands have **ecological benefits** too: preventing coastal erosion, filtering out pollutants, and absorbing some of the wave energy of storm surges caused by hurricanes.

There's nothing of any interest to tourists, but you have to

SIGHTS

OBSERVING THE ANIMALS

One of the greatest thrill in Guatemala is the chance to **see wild animals** going about their daily business in the forest. If you spend some time in one or more of the parks and preserves, your chances of seeing some critters are good. However, some animals are much more easily seen than others, and some visitors have unrealistic expectations.

White-nosed **coatis** (locally known as *pizotes*) are frequently seen, and they are friendly and fun. **Monkeys** are everyone's favorites, and they are pretty common (a little too common, say the owners of stolen sunglasses and hats). Guatemala has sevenspecies of monkeys: black-handed spider, white-faced capuchins, Geoffrey's tamarins, rufous-naped tamarins, night (owl) monkeys, squirrel and mantled howler monkeys, whose cries boom through the forest.

We'd all love to see a **wild cat**, and Guatemala has six species: pumas, oncilla, jaguars, ocelots, margays and jaguarundis. Outside of a zoo or. rehabilitation center, however, you're unlikely to spot one of these secretive, nocturnal predators.

If you really want to see some of the rarer forest denizens, visit one of the more remote parks, walk quietly, and take your hikes in the early morning or just before dusk. **I highly recommend hiring a local guide**, who can show you animals (and plants) that you would never see on your own.

go through there to get to the wonderful **Biotopo Punta de Manabique.** The park is on a remote peninsula sticking out into the Caribbean near Puerto Barrios. It is hard to get to, and has little in the way of lodging, but there are almost **untouched white sand beaches** and undisturbed *arribadas* of **turtles** coming ashore to lay their eggs. This is one of the best and least-visited wild areas in Guatemala. Difficult to access, it is the main reason to visit Guatemala's Caribbean coast.

The park is run by the obscure **FUNDARY** which offers a very few, very basic rooms in their research facility. You can hire a boat from Puerto Barrios to take you out and back, but expect to pay around $200 for this. If you can, try to arrange things through the hard-to-reach FUNDARY. Bird watchers and back-water kayakers will love the area. I am anxious to return!

Info: www.guate.net/fundary manabique/paquetes.htm; Tel. 502-948-0435.

BEST SLEEPS & EATS

The Caribbean side of Guatemala lacks high-quality, multi-star lodging. There are plenty of comfortable and stylish hotels and lodges but things are more basic than in other parts of the country.

LIVINGSTON
Villa Caribe $$
This is, by a slight margin, the nicest hotel in town. Some of the

rooms have spectacular views of the river mouth and the pool is quite nice. I love the pool. The rooms are comfortable but just. Water pressure is low and hot water is scarce. Other than that, the service is rather slow-slow. But almost all of the service in Livingston is slow-slow. Skip the restaurant except for breakfast. *Info: Livingston. www.villasdeguatemala.com; Tel. 502-7947-0072.*

SLEEPS & EATS

Posada El Delfin $$$

Built on a dock out into the bay, the 20-room Delfin is basic but is a good choice. It is in a quiet location. Rooms are largish with ceiling fans and wall air conditioners. Water pressure and temperature can be iffy, but other than that things are clean and neat. The restaurant is up on stilts out a ways into the river mouth with great views. The hotel frequently hosts groups of government officials, NGOs and church groups. The owner, Gus, knows Gay Talese and Erica Jong from his time living in New York and often hosts them during the cold months. Wi-fi is available. *Info: Livingston. www.posadaeldelfin.com; Tel. 502-7947-0694.*

Restaurante Margot $$

This is the place to go if you want to sample the local specialties *tepesqüintle* and wild turkey. They don't have much in the way of ambiance but it is clean and service is polite. Certainly not what you might expect to see on the menu in Ardmore, do not pass up the local specialty *tepesqüintle*. This is a small furry local animal prepared as a stew with chunks of "meat." It is reminiscent of pork chops. Delicious! If you must, this is also one of the best places to enjoy *langosta*, a local lobster-like dish. *Info: Livingston, at the North end of Calle Principal.*

Sandwich Shop $

Right across the street from the Posada El Delfin, this tiny hole in the wall features a window where you place your order and three plastic tables on the side of the street where you can enjoy breakfasts, smoothies and sandwiches. Their interesting menu has a few items on it that they actually have available. Ask what's on for the day. *Info: Livingston, Calle Marcos Sánchez Díaz.*

Bugamama $$

Bugamama has a great location right by the soccer field, with some tables overlooking the street and some overlooking the river mouth. It's very peaceful and the food is okay. The restaurant is run by **Sustainable Tourism School of Asociación Ak' Tenamit**, a Mayan NGO serving Mayan communities located around four protected areas in the Río Dulce region. All the employees are local tourism students learning how to run a restaurant. Unfortunately for the service, that is exactly what they are doing: *learning how to run a restaurant.* Service is friendly but glacial. No worries! They usually have a small portion of the extensive menu available. About 15 minutes after you are expecting to receive your food, you will sometimes see a waiter strip off his apron and run into town to buy an item necessary to produce the meal you ordered a half hour ago. You should eat here anyway since all profits go to a good cause. Pasta is your best bet. *Info: Livingston near the dock. Tel. 502-7842-5497.*

Tilingo Lingo $

The captivating Maria is owner and fascinating conversation partner at this memorable restaurant. She is Mexican and spent 10 years living in India. She is also a spectacular cook. The combination of Caribbean, Guatemalan, Mexican, and Indian influences leads to some amazing dishes. Try the whole curried fish. The ambiance is

LOCAL SPECIALTIES!

A couple of flavorful local specialties are not to be missed. **Tepesqüintle** is a small furry animal similar to a raccoon, prized by the locals above all food, except chicken. Wild turkey, **pava**, is another local favorite. It's hard to pass up **langosta**, local lobster, or crawfish. These are not like the ones from Maine with huge claws, but are like Florida lobsters with delicious tails. Realize however that they are endangered locally due to overfishing. The locals cannot resist the high price tourists will pay for the delicacy and entice them out of their holes with bleach, various poisons or explosives. Most are caught, cooked and eaten well before egg-bearing age. If a female is caught loaded with roe, the eggs are thrown away and the would-have-been mama sold to the tourist restaurants. I suggest avoiding this local delicacy if you like to feel good about your consumption habits.

what I have to call "very funky." It's all the way at the end of Calle Principal where the street just goes on down into the water and disappears like a boat ramp. Take one of the two tables outside and you can gaze across the bay to Belize. *Info: Livingston, at the North end of Calle Principal.*

SLEEPS & EATS

RÍO DULCE
Tortugal $$$

Right on the river and best reached by launch, the very tranquil Tortugal is the best lodging option in the area. They have a wide variety of rooms from backpacker specials with shared baths to freestanding bungalows with kitchens and all facilities needed for independent travelers to take care of their own needs. Their lovely restaurant and bar has great views of the river, and is popular with yachties and other expats. They have 20 rooms and slips for 50 yachts. There is no AC but the ceiling fans are adequate most of the time. *Info: Río Dulce. www.tortugal.com; Tel. 502-5306-6432.*

Sundog Café $$
This is probably the most popular place for expats to hang out. They serve hot and cold sandwiches and cold beer. It looks a little rough but go ahead on in anyway. The whole town looks a little rough. *Info: Río Dulce, Calle 1. Tel. 502-5529-0829.*

NO SHOPPING
None to speak of, anyway. The Caribbean towns offer little in the way of shopping that tourists would be interested in. Río Dulce is the place to buy yacht supplies.

11. PRACTICAL MATTERS

ARRIVALS & DEPARTURES
Flying to Guatemala
La Aurora International Airport (GUA) is right in the middle of Guatemala City. All of the international flights arrive there. It's new and modern, loaded with glitterati-type duty free shops. Flights within Guatemala almost all leave from the same airport. Most flights from North America and Europe arrive in the afternoon. Try to arrive early enough to leave yourself time to get to your destination before dark. Taxis to the city cost from $5 to $10. A shuttle from the airport to Antigua takes about an hour and another two and a half hours or so more to Panajachel. Ground transportation can be slow and is subject to unexpected long delays, so plan accordingly.

Flights to Guatemala tend to funnel through Atlanta, Miami, Houston, Mexico City and Los Angeles.

Cruises
Numerous cruise lines target Guatemala. Some lines stop for a day in Livingston or Ixtapa and offer quick tours to Antigua, the market at Chichi and the ruins at Tikal.

Celebrity Cruise Line
Tel. 800-722-5941
www.celebrity.com
Ships leave from Fort Lauderdale and San Francisco.

Norwegian Cruise Line
Tel. 800-327-7030
www.ncl.com
Nice ships leave from Miami and Los Angeles.

Regent Seven Seas Cruises
Tel. 877-505-5370
www.rssc.com
Regent (formerly Radisson) is the Rolls Royce of cruise lines. Their 14- and 16-night cruises leave from Ft. Lauderdale and San Francisco. Some trips include Los Angeles.

Zegrahm Expeditions
Tel. 800-628-8747
www.zeco.com
Zegrahm offers an eco-oriented itinerary aboard the 80-passenger Levant that includes Belize, Honduras, Costa Rica, and Panama.

GETTING AROUND GUATEMALA

By Air

There is not much in the way of internal air service in Guatemala. Tikal is really the only destination with scheduled service. Small charter flights to Cobán, Puerto Barrios and Puerto San José can be had, and charter helicopter service is available to almost anywhere. This is an expensive option but, if you don't want to endure the brutal, death-defying three hour winding-through-the-mountains drive from Guatemala City to the lake Atitlán area, a helicopter is the way to go.

Scheduled 20-minute flights from Guatemala City to Flores (base for exploring Tikal) cost around $275.

Some of the planes are a little on the creaky side and are definitely not up to high US standards, but accidents are rare. I have been in several where I could see light around the edges of the door and feel a draft after taking off. This was fine since the AC didn't work very well anyway. Some remote lodges are accessible only by landing on short, dirt runways in jungle clearings. This is part of why they call it "adventure travel."

By Boat

Remote lodges along both coasts and on Lake Atitlán often use small water taxis (*lanchas*), or fiberglass boats to bring guests to and from the mainland. Usually this is fine. Most of the boats have awnings, and the water is usually calm.

However, especially in the Livingston area, some of this type of transportation takes place in small, beat-up, leaky boats with dodgy-looking outboards. Lifejackets are not usually considered to be standard equipment. Paddles, anchors, and fire extinguishers also may not be in evidence. Sometimes little attempt is made to keep luggage dry. You are very likely to get at least some spray and, from time to time, you can get absolutely drenched. I have traveled to some lodges in boats with no paddles, anchors, life preservers or radios. If this bothers you, some of your travel options will be limited.

Using small *lanchas* is by far the best way to explore the villages around Lake Atitlán. I find they are always equipped with life jackets and are, overall, better than I have seen in other areas.

By Car

Driving yourself around the country provides flexibility and convenience. Main roads are generally pretty good but roads in isolated areas can be amazingly bad. You may want to consider a four-wheel-drive vehicle. High clearance is really the most important part. If you rent a small, compact sedan, you will probably find yourself bottoming out in large, pond-sized mud puddles and cow-sized potholes. At these times simply grit your teeth and hope you don't puncture the oil pan.

Driving anywhere in the country at night is simply not wise. I also suggest you do not drive in Guatemala City—day or night. Driving in the city is simply too much of a hassle; there are very few street signs and the traffic is intense. Stop signs and lights are routinely ignored. "Inventive" maneuvers like passing on the wrong side of the road with a huge, overloaded truck coming are common. Even if you consider yourself to be an excellent, defensive driver you may learn a

thing or two driving in Guatemala City. Taxis are cheap and convenient.

The main intercity roads in Guatemala are either paved or being worked on. Although road construction seems to be going on in many locations, rural roads can be some of the worst anywhere in the world. Washouts (*derrumbes*) are common, which may mean that the road you've been following on the map might not actually go where you want to go anymore.

Road signs are rare. Signs identifying small villages or large towns are just about nonexistent. At some rural crossroads, you may see a sign far down one branch. Drive down and look at it, as it may have relevant information. Realize that many locals standing by the side of the road have no more idea how to get to the next village than you do. Best to ask shuttle drivers, cops or truck drivers. Gas station attendants are another possible source for road information. Ask more than one person and ask often. Conflicting directions are part of the adventure.

By Car Rental or Private Driver

The best way to enjoy a short stay in Guatemala City is to hire an English-speaking driver. You can hire almost any cab in town for $10 an hour, but most drivers speak only fair English, if any. I suggest you call Raul Rodas (Tel. 502-5775-8276) for a very professional Spanish-speaking driver, or Rene and Francisca at Posada Belén, who can arrange for a local driver with excellent English. The charge is around $12 an hour but it's worth it.

I've used several of their drivers and had a great time. Their English was very good and they took me to all sorts of places I would never think of on my own. It's almost cheaper and much less hassle than renting a car.

Info: Guatemala City. Tel. 502-2253-4530.

If you must rent a car, there are several car companies at the airport in Guatemala City and in major tourist towns. Just across the street from the arrivals terminal, there is a large compound with a dozen or so car rental agencies. As you walk in with your baggage, rental agents will come out of their offices to encourage you to give them a try. You can play them off against each other if you have the energy but most will have similar prices. If the one you select does not have a nice clean, fairly new car, ask around the other offices.

I simply look in the lot for a car that appeals to me and ask whichever rental company has it what they want for it by the week. And away we go. The process may sound chaotic, and it is, but you can be in and out within 15 minutes or so. Prices run around $30 to $40 per day for a small compact, all in. Not bad.

It is usually not possible to take cars rented in Guatemala into Belize, Honduras, Mexico or otherwise out of the country. Some agencies insist that all drivers be at least 25 years old. Extra collision insurance may be required and some companies will not accept your US insurance. Rental car coverage provided by credit cards is also not always accepted. Small local agencies may offer similar service to the big names. I usually do not book in advance, preferring to choose my agency by deciding which one seems to have the nicest (newest, fewest dents) car when I show up.

Guatemala Renta Autos
Aurora International Airport
Tel. 502-2329-9040
www.guatemalarentacar.com

Budget
Aurora International Airport
Tel. 502-2332-7744
www.budgetcentroamerica.com/guatemala/

Alamo
Aurora International Airport
Tel. 502-2362-2701
www.alamoguatemala.com

By Taxi
Taxis in Guatemala are cheap, cheap, and cheap. You can go almost anywhere within most cities for $2-$3. With a little bargaining, you can rent cabs for $10 to $12 an hour. There are no meters. As you should do anywhere, always ask the price before getting into the cab. There is usually little or no haggling. Resist the urge to tip. It's just not done in Guatemala, and fares are usually an exact dollar amount: $1 or $2, so you won't be tempted to round up.

There are zillions of taxis zooming around and you will find them honking at you more or less annoyingly as you walk around. Wave your arms about to indicate your need. Sharing taxi rides with strangers is common. Just because a cab appears to have a fare already doesn't mean you should not try to flag it down. Not all are air-conditioned. When it rains, all the taxis are full.

By Tuk-Tuk
These wonderful inventions, common in Asia, are three-wheeled taxis that can just about squeeze in three gringos with a modicum of luggage. They are rough, bouncy and slow, but cheaper than taxis. You flag them down in the usual way (wave your arms around frantically). Determine the price for your destination before getting in. When it rains, all the tuk-tuks are full.

By Bus
Colorful and cheap, converted yellow Blue Bird school buses (*camionetas*) seem to be everywhere. You can just flag them down or wait at a marked bus stop. An attendant passes through the bus from time to time collecting the modest fare. These famous **chicken buses** (so named since your seat mates may actually *be* chickens) are almost always jam-packed, are not air-conditioned, and are not really practical if you have much luggage. Seats in these buses were designed to hold the butts of three school children. In Latin America they routinely hold the butts of three adults.

There is no doubt that the wildest drivers, by far, are the chicken bus drivers. Terrible bus wrecks are daily occurrences. Robberies on buses in Guatemala City are also common. If you decide you are going to ride the chicken buses anyway, don't read the local *Diario* newspaper or watch the local evening news on TV. The best newspaper, *La Prensa Libre*, features bus crash photos on page 3 every day. The other major paper, *Diario* has little news *other* than bus crashes.

Most long-distance buses leave from their own terminals. You can get long-distance buses in Guatemala City for destinations all over the country. These buses tend to be modern, air-conditioned and relatively comfortable. They also tend to be jampacked, with many people standing in the crowded aisles. Their radios, tuned to mind-numbing pop stations, are usually cranked up to ear-splitting volume. Luggage can be put on the roof rack. The long-distance buses are efficient, cheap and fast. Most destinations within the country are less than $10.

The best buses, known as "Pullmans," are large, often double-decker jobs with good AC, comfortable seats and TV blaring out cheesy C-level, five-year-old action movies. Seats are usually assigned. Views from the front seats on the top floor are spectacular but sometimes frightening since you also have the best view of your driver's wild-assed driving habits and the plunging abysses at the edge of the highway (no guardrails). Fun!

By Tourist Shuttle

Most tourists find themselves being hauled around in shuttles, largish vans that hold around 12 people or so. You can book these shuttles through your hotel or from any of the kiosks/travel agents you see all over the place. Prices vary widely for the same trip. You can sometimes bargain for a lower price when booking through smaller agencies. Departure times are scheduled in advance, although they sometimes arrive early and get irritated if you are not ready. It is also not unusual for the shuttles to arrive an hour or two late (or even more) with no apology other than a shrug and a grin.

The higher-priced shuttles go around town picking people up at their hotels and dropping them off the same way at the arrival destination. Prices range from a cheap $6 to go from Guatemala City to Antigua to over $30 for long hauls.

As you walk around you will see a variety of agencies offering the same trip for wildly different prices. The price you pay often has little to do with the quality of the service. You may book a trip with a small agency for $5 and find yourself in a nice, newish shuttle from one of big name companies where the other passengers all paid $12 for the same trip. Or you may find yourself in a cramped, beat up older shuttle with dodgy-looking tires. If you go ahead and pay top dollar at one of the better agencies, you are much more likely to end up in a nice van.

These conveyances are usually modern and safe. However, many lack seatbelts, spare tires or tire tread. They don't *usually* pack them too full. This is actually the best way to get around the country.

Realize that road conditions in Guatemala can be uncertain. Construction, washouts, small riots can all cause huge delays with traffic backed up for miles. Be sure to build plenty of flexibility into your schedule. Don't think you can do tight, just-in-time scheduling.

Atitrans is one of the better services. They run shuttles on all the main routes, including from the airport in Guatemala City to Antigua and Panajachel. They also offer trips to the market at Chichi on Thursdays and Sundays.

Info: Calle Santander next to Hotel Regis, Panajachel. www.atitrans.com; Tel. 502-7762-0152. 6a Avenida sur No. 8, Antigua. Tel. 502-7832-3371.

By Pickup Truck Collective

You will see hundreds of small pickup trucks (*picops*) running around with seemingly hundreds of locals crammed in back with their bundles, chickens, goats, kids, bicycles, etc. This is the cheapest way of getting somewhere. For a short ride into town from your hotel, if you don't have much luggage, it is certainly an option to consider. The cost is usually just the equivalent of a nickel or a dime. Just wave your arm when you see one coming and hop in the back. Ask the price first. You usually pay when you get off.

BASIC INFORMATION
Banking & Changing Money

The Guatemalan currency is known as the **quetzal**. Bills come in Q1, Q5, Q10, Q20, Q50, and

Q100 denominations. Unfortunately, even though the bills are beautiful, with depictions of great Guatemalan leaders and all, most are faded, well-worn and hard to tell apart. The twenties and fives are both sort of blue in color and look identical in dim light. The one hundred Quetzal bill has a symbol prominently displayed that strongly resembles a "10." So it would be easy for a gringo like me to have trouble telling them apart in a dark bar without my glasses. Pay attention.

Q1 coins are common. Occasionally, you will run into *centavos*, coins that are not useful for much of anything. Like US dimes and nickels, Guatemalan 25 centavo coins are larger than the 50 centavo coins. I find deserving beggars accept the small coins gratefully.

Many tourist-oriented places will take your dollars but will usually give you your change in *quetzales*, at a convenient rate (for them). You probably won't need to change at the airport on arrival, since most taxi drivers will be happy with dollars and will round up the fare to the closest dollar amount or even quote you the fare in dollars upfront.

Banks can be slow and bureaucratic. Avoid them if possible. ATMs (*cajeras automáticas*) usually offer the best exchange rate, even after the credit card clearing companies take a small slice of the action. However, you will encounter numerous ATMs that simply don't work, or won't work with your card the particular day you need them to. Inoperative ATMS seem to be more common than ones that work. Get cash before the weekend, since many ATMs break down or run out of money by Saturday afternoon. They don't tend to get fixed or reloaded until Monday afternoon.

Be sure to notify your bank and credit card companies ahead of time that you are going to Guatemala so they don't block your card the first time you try to use it (they'll probably block it anyway). It's not rare to have to call the 800 number on the back of your card to reassure them it is actually you in Guatemala using your card as you told them you would be. Keep a couple of hundred bucks in cash minimum at all times if possible, and keep two or three credit/debit cards going. Don't let yourself get too low on money.

Plan Ahead for Credit Card Trouble

I am always careful to call my credit card companies before any overseas trip alerting them to my plans to use their cards in some strange place, like Guatemala. They always thank me for telling them and assure me they have made a note of it in the computer and that there will be no problems. In spite of this they almost always block my cards as soon as they realize someone is trying to use them in such an outlandish place and I have to call them a second time (expensively) to get them to unblock the cards.

MasterCard, and particularly Visa, are accepted widely but be sure to ask in advance. If you are visiting more remote areas be sure to have cash in small denominations handy. Many local restaurants and other businesses work with cash only. Try to keep a supply of small bills on hand. It may seem strange, but many businesses, especially small street stands, are simply not capable of changing a Q100 note.

You can get a cash advance on your card at some banks. **Banco Industrial** seems to be the most likely to perform this service in most towns. Wait in line to speak to one of the nice young ladies at the desk and then, after they work their complicated magic, you can proceed to wait in the line for the teller windows where you exchange your paperwork for a wad of *quetzales*. Allow an hour or so for this.

Business Hours

Guatemala operates to US standards for working hours. Commercial entities open around 8 or 9 and close around 5 or 6. Restaurants generally start serving lunch around 12 and dinner around 6, but don't be surprised if no one but you arrives until after 8 or so. Some bars and clubs don't get going or even open their doors until well after midnight. Call first.

Climate & Weather

Even though it is close to the equator, Guatemala enjoys a relatively temperate climate. **The Caribbean side is hot and muggy** with little in the way of cooling breezes. **The Pacific coast is also hot but a steady wind almost always blows**, cooling things off nicely. The central highlands, where you find most touristic attractions, are always cool and pleasant with few annoying bugs. Temperatures rarely get above 80° F in the daytime or below 60° at night, as much of the country is at relatively high, cool altitudes or subject to cooling trade winds. Even so, it can get quite humid and you can soak a shirt through with sweat walking around in the lowlands on a summer afternoon. You might want a light jacket or sweater if you spend time in the highlands. I've seen locals all bundled up with mittens on, shivering as if they were in North Dakota in January. If you don't believe me, after you get there, you can buy a cheap jacket or sweater in a used clothing store (*paca*) or stall for $1 or $2. (That's where all the old clothes you donate to the needy end up being sold.)

Rain is part of the fun. Rainy season runs more or less from May to December, but conditions vary quite a bit due to local circumstances. Tropical downpours can be intense but rarely last long. Weeks and weeks of steady rain are not common. Short, intense, afternoon rainsqualls are the norm. They usually just serve to cool things down a bit.

It doesn't make much sense to plan a trip based on avoiding rain. There are several Guate-malan microclimates that may offer more or less rain than is usual across the country for the time you plan on visiting. It may be raining intensely in Antigua while Livingston suffers a dry spell.

It's not a bad idea to bring along an umbrella (*una para agua*).

Consulates & Embassies

Guatemala City is a thriving international hub for business, and sports embassies and consulates from over 150 countries.

The **United States Embassy** is a biggie. *(Avenida La Reforma. Tel. 502-2326-4000).* To contact the **Canadian Embassy**: *13 Calle 8-44 Zone 10, Edificio Edyma Plaza. Tel. 502-2363-4348.*

Electricity

Electric current and fixtures in Guatemala are pretty much the same as in the US. Plugs are usually two-prong and not grounded. You may want to bring along a three-prong-to-two-prong adapter, or just twist the ground prong off whatever appliance you simply must use. Remote lodges may run on generators or solar power. Some may turn the power off at night. This means you may not be able to run your laptop or hairdryer whenever you like. Blackouts are common in all parts of the country and can last for several hours. Most hotel rooms come with a candle and matches—just in case.

Emergencies & Safety

Guatemala doesn't have a proper 911 service, but you can call ASISTUR by dialing 1500 from anywhere in Guatemala and they will put you in touch with the necessary emergency services. Dialing 911 will also get you to an emergency services operator. Dialing 110 gets you the national police. 125 gets you the local Red Cross.

Crime

As in any country, you need to take care of yourself. There are thieves preying on the unwary all over the world and Guatemala is no different. Guatemala City suffers a harsh reputation for street crime. Stay in the center of town in the Zona Viva or in the Centro Histórico. Be careful. Avoid other parts of town. Just don't go there. There is nothing of interest there anyway. When you are out at night, take a taxi, door to door, to and from your destination. You can write down your taxi driver's phone number and call them to come and pick you up after eating, drinking or whatever other nighttime activity you get into.

Few visitors have any problem with crime, but it is a good idea to keep copies of your passport, a little cash and an extra credit card separate from the rest of your luggage. Use the in-room safes if provided by your hotel. Don't take up with strangers you meet on the street.

I have heard a couple of reports of tourists being targeted with "date rape drugs," but I hear similar reports in Knoxville, near where I live. Never leave your drinks unattended in a bar or restaurant while you visit the can. It is not a particularly good idea to accept offers of food from strangers.

If you mess around with any of the women you may casually meet in bars, casinos or night-clubs, you should use appropriate caution. Don't take all of your money with you on such excursions. If you bring dubious ladies back to your room, be sure to leave the bulk of your valuables in the safe or in a friend's room. These women know to look under the mattress for your stash.

Antigua and Panajachel each have a large police presence. Tourist police seem to be everywhere. This is a good thing. Like most Guatemalans, I find the cops to be generally friendly and helpful. *Estamos aquí para servirle*, we are here to serve you, is what they tell me when I ask them for directions.

Food

One of the most wonderful reasons to visit Guatemala is to eat. The combination of wide international influence, fresh local produce and seafood and plenty of tourists, well-off business types and retirees willing to pay means the country has plenty of truly great restaurants.

All the familiar North American fast food places are represented in Guatemala: McDonalds, Burger King and Subway are all over the place. Local fast food fried chicken chain **Pollo Campero** can be found in almost every town (and in Brazil, Spain, Texas, Boston and Dubai). If you want to know where the locals eat, at least those who have enough money to eat out from time to time, you will find them in the same chains you know and love so well back home enjoying the same cholesterol-laden burgers the locals back home in Springfield enjoy. Don't be ashamed. When it's time for a burger, it's time for a burger, wherever you are. Guatemalan kids, just like American kids, want to eat at McDonald's. This should be no surprise.

Restaurant prices in Guatemala are similar to US prices in upscale restaurants, but usually less in more modest places. However, the food is usually better in Guatemala. Fortunately, the country's infrastructure doesn't lend itself well to distributing and using lots of frozen food. So restaurants tend to actually cook things rather than just heat up things delivered by the Sysco truck as they do in the US. And the seafood and local fruits and vegetables are wonderful. Fruit juices area almost always fresh squeezed and inexpensive.

Be sure to try the local **típico** specialties. Some food choices will be similar to what you see in Mexican restaurants in the US. I love the **taquitos**, small tortillas filled with this or that, deep fried and served with guacamole. The local, tiny tortillas are almost always patted into shape by hand, and sometimes are made from blue corn.

Típico, or traditional Guatemalan food, is savory and interesting, based on local seafood, vegetables, and chicken. Small tortillas are typically served fresh three times a day. You will see ladies patting them up by hand, toasting them briefly on a hot *comal* and selling them to locals at *los tres tiempos*, breakfast, lunch and dinner. Rice and fried plantains (*plátanos*) are typical with breakfast. **Pipián**, a rich chicken stew with a sauce made of tomato and pumpkin seed, is probably the best known traditional Guatemalan dish, and is delicious. Look for **pupusas, tamales, chuchitos**, and **paches**—variations of corn-stuffed or corn-enwrapped goodies. Guatemalans like to have a cup of coffee and a piece of sweet cake in the afternoon. You'll see lots of little shops selling cookies and sweet bread. Go for it.

I hope you like **chicken**. Guatemala is the chicken-eatingest place I have ever visited. The ever-present fast food chicken outlet, *Pollo Campero*, seems to be everyone's favorite. Their restaurants are always clean and efficient, and are always packed with *Guatemaltecos* honking down the fried bird.

Smaller, remote restaurants may have elaborate menus with seafood, various types of steaks, pasta, chicken and other appetizing items on offer. Quite often, as you begin the ordering process, it comes to light that they actually don't have very many of the star attractions that feature on the menu. Each time you make another selection, the very polite waiter or waitress will tell you they don't have that today. When this happens, go for the chicken. They *always* have chicken.

Tourist restaurants charge much more than the places where most locals eat. Most locals can't afford to eat in regular restaurants. You'll see many people buying full meals on the street from ladies carrying their entire restaurants in baskets on their heads. Try this. I have been pleasantly surprised by the delicious, often unidentifiable stuff I've tried. Taco and fried chicken stands abound and are usually a good bet.

Shrimp, corvina (sea bass), **mojara** and **robalo** (snook) are good choices for local fish. I avoid mushy-textured tilapia wherever I go. **Black bass** is sometimes available in the Lake Atitlán area, and is a very good eating fish.

Fruits to look for include delicious tiny **sweet bananas, papayas, mangos, passion fruit, carambola, aguacate** and the weird but delicious **guanábana**. A sad trend I have noticed is for some restaurants catering to middle class, upwardly-mobile Guatemalans to serve instant coffee instead of ground, Sunny Delight instead of fresh squeezed orange juice, and toasted white bread instead of fresh tortillas. Some of these middle class *fresas* (strawberries) or yuppies scorn their roots and don't want to be seen consuming foods typically consumed by poor country people. Restaurants serving hot tortillas are either *comedores* aimed at poor working Guatemalans or tourist places aimed at rich gringos—the middle class wants white bread.

Service, although almost always friendly or even enthusiastic, is often much slower than what you may be used to in the States. This is partly because they are **actually cooking your food** instead of simply nuking something pre-prepared from the Sysco truck. If you want to have your drink arrive before the meal, you will need to specify that very clearly. The idea, normal in the US, that a diner should be served a drink immediately upon sitting down and pressed to order more throughout the meal, is missing in Guatemala. If you order a beer and a meal at the same time, you may well receive both at the same time—30 or 40 minutes after you sat down, having sat at an empty table for all that time. At breakfast, coffee may arrive with the meal or even afterwards, even though your head may be lying on the table and loud groans escaping from your caffeine-deficient body. One reason for this is that most waiters, cooks, managers and restaurant owners can rarely, if ever, afford to eat in restaurants themselves. They simply do not know the fine points of service. They have not personally experienced poor or good service in restaurants.

Health
You do not need any special inoculations or shots before visiting Guatemala. Malaria is pretty much a thing of the past but, if you plan on spending more than a month or so in remote areas like Petén, it would be a good idea to take prophylactic pills. Drinking water from the tap is

not a good idea in most places. Hotels filter their tap water or offer guests purified water (*agua mineral* or *agua pura*) in their rooms. Use condoms, dummy. AIDS, known internationally as SIDA, certainly exists in Guatemala, as do other loathsome venereal diseases.

Hospitals

Although it is inexpensive, Guatemala's health care is not of top quality. Some visitors come to Guatemala for medical reasons but it is not one of the countries known as a medical tourism destination. There is a decent hospital in Guatemala City.

Info: Hospital Centro Medico, Guatemala City. 6a Avenida 3-47, one 10. Tel. 502-2332-3555.

Etiquette

In general, Guatemalans pay more attention to the social niceties than do North Americans. It is important to say at least *"buenas"* whenever you encounter someone and *"adiós"* when you part. It is more polite to say the whole phrase, though: *buenos días, buenas tardes,* or *buenas noches.* Inquiring after someone's health or how they passed the night is always appreciated.

LADIES - COVER UP!
Leave the shorts and sexy tops for the nightclub, beach or hotel pool. Although Guatemalan men will be pleased to look over your assets wherever you display them, local women do not usually wear revealing clothing, especially outside the larger towns.

When boarding a bus or sitting down in a crowded restaurant it is nice to say *"buenas"* to those around you. Except in large cities, it is common to say *"buenos días"* to strangers when walking down the street (adults). This isn't done in the US but, in Guatemala, people may think you are stuck up if you don't at least smile and acknowledge their presence. In general, people in Guatemala are quite friendly to strangers. It is normal to strike up a casual conversation with seatmates or others around you. This is good: you can ask questions of the locals you encounter without feeling too nosy.

When beginning a meal or if you encounter someone already eating, it is polite to say *"buen provecho,"* (have a nice meal). Guatemalans almost always dress better than Americans do.

If you see someone in sweats, shorts or t-shirt, it is usually a gringo. This does not mean you have to wear a tie at dinner, but it does mean you should attempt to dress a little better than you might be inclined to on vacation. Locals just shake their heads at gringos wearing tank tops, halter tops, shorts and sandals with socks. Shiny leather shoes and tucked-in shirts are normal for men in town—dresses or conservative slacks for women. Guatemalan businessmen in the city wear ties, and are usually better dressed than their US counterparts.

T-back or thong bathing suits are acceptable at large tourist hotel pools, but going topless is not something that is approved of in Guatemala. To be comfortable, check out your fellow guests at the pool before appearing in your extremely skimpy bathing outfit. Such bathing suits don't take up much space in your luggage, so go ahead and pack one, just in case.

Further Reading
John Kircher, *A Neotropical Companion*. Princeton University Press, 1999.
Daniel Wilkinson, *Silence on the Mountain*. Duke University Press, 2004

Bonny Dilger, *Blood in the Cornfields*. Publish America, 2005.
Richard Morgan Szybist, *The Lake Atitlán Reference Guide*. Adventures in Education, 2004.
Elizabeth Bell, *Antigua Guatemala: the City and its Heritage*. Antigua Tours, 2005.

Internet Access
Wireless Internet access, wi-fi, is now available in almost all hotels in the world. Guatemala is no different. Unfortunately, wi-fi technology is still fairly new, so in many hotels the world over, perhaps most, the connections are poor or unavailable anywhere a little distant from the lobby (like in your room). I find this is true in the US as well.

Internet cafés abound but you probably won't need to visit one if your hotel has a decent connection. Most hotels have computers with connections available for guests.

Language
Spanish is the national language and is spoken without the heavy accents of nearby Venezuela or Cuba. The country is known for speaking fairly pure *Castellano*. Guatemalans do not tend to cut words short as some Central Americans do. Most Guatemalans will insist they don't really have any local slang but may

admit to using a few slang expressions from Mexico.

In addition to Spanish, there are 24 different languages in daily use in Guatemala. There are 22 Mayan dialects used; Garífuna is spoken in the Caribbean areas and Xinca (pronounced "shinca") is an unusual leftover from a unique group of 15th-century immigrants from an obscure part of Spain.

Newspapers & Magazines

There are several dailies published in Guatemala City. The best by far is **La Prensa** (www.prensa.com), a Spanish-language daily with a tremendous amount of pages each week devoted to travel, tourism and gruesome automobile and bus accidents. Their editorials are unrestrained. **Diario**, the rival daily, features even more up-close, full-color photographs of the daily bus wrecks and street murders. A shapely, naked female bum graces a full inside page every day, often with no caption or explanation for its presence.

There are a couple of English-language tourist publications. Look for the **Revue** (www.revuemag.com), a monthly aimed at tourists, loaded with articles and ads of interest to visitors. **Que Pasa en Antigua** (www.grupoquepasa.com) comes out twice a month and lists all the best happy hours and live music happenings in town.

Maps

There are several decent road maps available. The most common one is actually a tourist map that is so full of tiny little markings for the various sites that it can hardly be read at all. The best one to get is the plastic-coated **International Travel Map Guatemala** (www.itmb.com). You can buy one from Amazon.

Passport & Visa Regulations

Americans and Canadians are required to have valid passports and are entitled to stay in the country for 30 days. Tourist stays can be extended for an additional 60 days with a little bit of hassle. Go to the Immigration Office (*Migración*), to make this happen.

Postal Service

The best way to think about the postal service in Guatemala is to pretend that they just don't have any. Courier services are the way things move about the country. Official post office boxes are almost unobtainable, so mailbox centers thrive. Bills are usually paid in person at banks. Many tourist operations have mail forwarding services based in Miami that forward regular mail by courier. Stamps are purchased mainly in post offices—few hotels seem to have them available for guests.

Telephones

Regular landline phones work just about as they do in the US. But phone numbers have eight digits. Don't think about it. Just dial. The best thing to do is simply to buy a cheap cell phone when you arrive in the country. You can buy a cheap one for about $20 from a stall, then fill it with talk time by purchasing phone cards (tarjetas telefónicas) in small shops. Look for doble saldo (double charge) or triple saldo (triple charge) days for a real deal.

Mobile phones are the best and cheapest way to call within the country and for calls back to the US. The local mobile phone companies often have specials with double or triple minutes. **Tigo** and **Movistar** are the most popular. There is no Verizon, US Cellular or T-Mobile presence in the country, no matter what those companies may tell you.

A surprise to most gringos, mobile phone usage in Central America is dirt cheap compared with US rates. Rates vary but, basically, you can talk for hours for a couple of bucks. Calls to the US from Central America on mobile phones are a bargain. Hotels charge anywhere from a few cents to way north of $4.50 per minute for calls to the US.

US Phones in Guatemala

Most unlocked GSM phones work fine in Guatemala with the addition of a cheap local chip. If you buy a local chip, usually around $20, you will have a local number and your friends back home can easily call you at that number. From the US, dial 011-502-xxxx-xxxx. It's easy.

Your US cell phone company may be able to set you up with global roaming so that your regular US number will work in Guatemala. Such calls cost a foolish $4-6 per minute.

Be sure to call and have your phone unlocked (flasheado) in the US before you leave.

Many of the more remote parts of the country do not have cell coverage, but I am always surprised when my phone rings while I'm fishing 30 miles out in the Pacific or hiking miles back in a cloud forest.

Time

Guatemala runs on Central Standard Time (GMT−6) and does not do Daylight Savings. Guatemala is near the equator, so the length of day does not change much. It gets light at about 6am and gets dark about 6pm. It gets dark in a hurry too. There is not much in the way of dusk—it's daytime and then all of a sudden it's dark. Plan ahead.

Tipping
In general, Guatemalans are not the mad tippers Americans are. It is simply not necessary to tip cab drivers. The fares are almost always an even dollar or *quetzal* amount so you don't even need to round up. Many restaurants include a 10% service charge on the bill. Have a look or ask to see if this is so before forking over more dough. I tend to tip bartenders with each drink order, thinking I will get better service for subsequent orders if the bartender knows I'm ready to tip for good service. But don't spoil it for the rest of us. This is not the US, and people just do not tip very much. Except at large, tourist-oriented hotels, no one will be surprised or offended if you keep your change in your pocket.

Tourist Information
INGUAT (*Instituto Guatemalteca de Turismo*) is Guatemala's tourist agency. Their headquarters are in Guatemala City at 8a. Avenida 4-52, Zone 1. They also have an office at the airport and in most cities and towns around the country. Their role is to help tourists on their way. In reality they offer little more than a few glossy brochures but these can come in handy for figuring out what you want to do. Delightfully, dialing 1500 gets you an English-speaking person dedicated to helping tourists.

Water
Drinking water from the tap is not a good idea in most places. Hotels filter their tap water or offer guests purified water (*agua mineral* or *agua pura*) in their rooms. Most bars that are nice enough to have ice will use purified water to make it.

Weights & Measures
Guatemala, like many countries, is inching over to the metric system. Fuel is still sold by the gallon. Road signs and speed limits are in kilometers.

What to Bring
For gifts, garden and flower seeds (no foolin'), school supplies and postcards of your home town are usually greeted with smiles. A three-prong to two-prong electric plug adaptor is a good thing to throw in your suitcase (or just tear off the ground prong from whatever appliance you are attempting to plug in). An umbrella may come in handy, al-

though many hotels offer them for guest use.

Bring a light sweater or jacket. I know this is the tropics we are talking about here, but remember that most of the popular areas of the country are at surprisingly high altitudes and can get cool at night. If you don't believe me or just forget to bring something warm, you can buy a used sweatshirt at a *paca* (used clothing store) for a buck or two. Such stores are hugely popular. You can buy back the same clothes you donated to Goodwill a few months before. Local entrepreneurs buy these used cloths from the US bundled up on pallets (*pacas*) and sell them in local markets to eager Guatemalan buyers.

ESSENTIAL SPANISH
Pleasantries
A simple *"buenas"* works just fine for a casual *"hello"* or *"goodbye"* almost any time of day, but it is more polite to come out with the whole salutation: *buenos días, buenas tardes* or *buenas noches.*

Please – *por favor*
Thank you – *gracias*
You're welcome – *de nada*
Excuse me – *perdóneme, permiso* or *discúlpeme*
Good day – *buenos días*

Good night – *buenas noches*
Goodbye – *adiós*
Hello – *hola*
How are you? – *¿Cómo está Usted?* or *¿Qué tal?*
Fine – *muy bien*
Pleased to meet you – *mucho gusto*

Everyday Phrases
Yes – *sí*
No – *no*
I don't know. – *No sé.*
Do you speak English? – *¿Habla usted inglés?*
I don't speak Spanish. – *Yo no hablo español.*
Friend – *amigo*
Where? – *¿Dónde?*
When? – *¿Cuando?*
Why? – *¿Porqué?*
Because – *por qué*
How much? – *¿Cuanto?*
How do you say...? – *¿Cómo se dice...?*
Today – *hoy*
Tomorrow – *mañana*
Yesterday – *ayer*
I would like – *quisiera*
Here – *aquí*
There – *allá*
More – *más*
Less – *menos*
Much – *mucho*
Little – *poco*
Large – *grande*
Small – *pequeño*
Good – *bueno*
Bad – *malo*

Travel Terms

Airport – *(el) aeropuerto*
ATM – *cajeras automáticas*
Avenue – *(la) avenida*
Bank – *(el) banco*
Bathroom – *(el) baño, sanitario*
Boat – *(el) barco, bote*
Bus – *(el) autobús, camioneta*
Car – *(el) coche, carro*
Gas station – *(la) bomba, gasolinera*
Hotel – *(el) hotel*
How far is . . . ? – *¿Qué distancia es. . . ?*
Indians – *Indígenas.* It is not considered respectful to say "Indian."
Money – *(el) dinero*
Taxi – *(el) taxi*
Road, highway – *(la) carretera*
Street – *(la) calle*

Eating & Drinking

Apple – *(la) manzana*
Banana – *(el) banano*
Barbeque – *(la) parilla*
Beef – *(el) bistec*
Beer – *(la) cerveza*
Black coffee – *café negro, café natural*
Bottled water – *agua mineral* or *agua pura*
Bread – *(el) pan*
Cheese – *(el) queso*
Chicken – *(el) pollo*
Coffee – *(el) café*
Coffee with milk – *café con leche*
Delicious – *delicioso*
Drunk – *borracho*
Fish – *(el) pescado*

Fruits – *(las) frutas*
Garlic – *(el) ajo*
Glass of water – *un vaso de agua*
Glass of wine – *una copa de vino*
Guacamole – *(el) guacamol*
Guava – *(la) guayaba*
Ham – *(el) jamón*
Have a nice meal – *buen provecho*
Juice – *(el) jugo*
Lemon, lime – *(el) limón*
Liver – *(el) hígado*
Marinated seafood salad – *(el) ceviche*
Meat – *(la) carne*
Menu – *(el) menú, lista*
Milk – *(la) leche*
Octopus – *(el) pulpo*
Orange – *(la) naranja*
Pineapple – *(la) piña*
Plantain – *(el) plátano*
Pork – *(el) cerdo*
Potato – *(la) papa*
Raw – *crudo*
Red wine/white wine – *vino tinto / vino blanco*
Salad – *(la) ensalada*
Sea bass – *(la) corvina*
Seafood – *(los) mariscos*
Shrimp – *(los) camarones*
Smoothie, milkshake – *(el) batido, licuado*
Snapper – *(el) pargo*
Snook – *(el) robalo*
Soft drink – *(el) refresco*
Tea – *(el) té*
Tuna – *(el) atún*
Vegetables – *(las) legumbres*
Water – *(el) agua*

Slang (*Chapinismos*)

A toda madre! – That's great, that's bitchin'! You will hear this often but probably should not try to use it yourself.

A gato viejo, ratón tierno – for an old cat, a young mouse

¡*A todo dar!* – Bitchin'! Great!

Agarrado – tightwad

Agarre – fling or affair

Agringado – Americanized (a person)

¡*Aguas!* – Look out! (Here comes the boss.)

Asientos – the runs (shits)

Babosadas – lies or foolishness

Beneficio – coffee factory

Bochinche – gossip

Bohío – thatched hut, often a small beachfront restaurant or bar

Borracho – drunk

Bolo – a little drunk

Cachito – a little bit

Cada cabeza es un mundo – each to his own

Canche – blond person

Cantar – to take a poop. *Fue a cantar,* He went to take a poop

Caquero – snob or rich person

Casera – mistress

Catracho – someone from Honduras (not derogatory)

Cervecear – to drink a cold one

Chapín, Chapines – Guatemalan(s) (not derogatory)

Capitalinos – citizens of Guatemala City

Chavo (a) – young guy, girl

Chimona, ¡*Qué chimona!* – slut, What a slut!

Chonte – cop or flatfoot

Chucho – mutt (dog)

Chupar – to drink

Clavos – problems

Colectivo – a collective van or boat

Condongo – condom

Cruda (tengo una) – I am hung over

Cuates – pals, cronies

Culón – big ass

Dinerito – coins, bribe

Echar un palo – to blow your wad

Espanglish – Spanglish

Estadounidense – someone from the United States

Fichas – coins

Flaco (a) – skinny

Fría – beer

Fulano – guy, some guy

Garífuna – Caribbean culture

Goma (estar de) – hung over

Gringo(a) – European or North American (not derogatory)

Guanaco – someone from El Salvador (not derogatory)

Guaro – local cane liquor

Güicoy – gay (homosexual)

Huevón – lazy person

Patrulla trulla – cop car

Hijo de cien mil putas – son of a bitch

Hora Americana – more or less on time

Indígenas – indigenous – it is not in good taste to say Indians or *Indios*

Mango, mangazo – good looking guy, muscular

Mano – bro', ¡oye mano! – hey bro'

Mañoso – pervert

Mara – youth gang

Mero mero – big boss

Miércoles – poo

Mordida – bribe

Mota – marihuana

¡Órale! – See you later dude! Okay, catch you later.

Panza verde – a native of Antigua, literally, "green belly"

Papacito, papito – hot or sexy guy

Papos – rolling papers

Parrandero(a) – party animal

Pintar – sow your seed, make babies

Pisto – money

Popó – poop

Porfa – please, very informal

¡Púchica! – Great! Holy cow!

¡A Púchica! – Oh damn!

Qué te vaya bien – have a nice trip

¿Qué onda vos?– What's up dude?

Ratero – pickpocket

Sendero – nature trail

Shuco – dirty

¡Tas buena mamí! – You're lookin' good, baby!

Trago – a shot (of rum)

Trincarse – to make out. Me trinque con una mujer bonita. – I made out with a pretty woman.

Vos – dude

Pronunciation

It's important to have a basic idea of pronunciation, so that you can at least pronounce place names correctly. Spanish is a phonetic language, meaning that words are almost always spelled just as they sound. Knowing a few rules helps.

Vowels are pronounced roughly as follows:

a – as in father

e – is always pronounced "a" as we pronounce a long "a". Pedro is pronounced Paydro rather than Peedro

i – as in magazine

o – as in phone

u – as in prune

There are no silent vowels. For example, coche (car) is pronounced KO-chay. A written accent on a vowel means that it is stressed, as in Colón (ko-LONE).

Consonants are pronounced roughly the same as in English, except:

c – like k before a, o or u; like s before e or i

h – always silent

j – like h in home

ll – like y in yet

ñ – like ni in union

z – like s in sink

INDEX

TravelNotes

Things Change!
Phone numbers, prices, addresses, quality of service – all change. If you come across any new information, let us know. No item is too small! Contact us at :

jopenroad@aol.com
or
www.openroadguides.com

PHOTO CREDITS

Front cover photo: John Pavelka (flickr). *Back cover photo:* Chensiyuan (wikimedia).

The following photos are from wikimedia commons: p. 128: Shark; p. 130: Doug Janson.

The following photos are from Bruce Morris (brucemorris.com: pp. 2, 8, 55, 57, 58, 59, 60, 61, 67, 70, 73, 75, 76, 85, 88, 90, 91, 98, 105, 107, 116, 158, 192, 195, 197, 200.

The following photos are from www.guate360com: p. 157,

The following images are from flickr.com: p. 1: Island Spice; p. 3 top: Fernando Reyes Palencia; p. 3 middle: dibaer; pp. 3 bottom, 168: Jeff Prod; p. 9: Cesar Aguilar; pp. 10, 120, 132 bottom, 134, 137, 142, 146, 150, 152: Adal-Honduras; p. 11: A.www.viajar24h.com; p. 12 left: krlitoxgt; p. 12 right: MikeMurga; p. 14: Greg and Annie; p. 17: Oscar Mota; p. 19: magnusfranklin; pp. 21, 30, 34 bottom: Laura Calverley; p. 22: Gorski; pp. 24, 86, 93: toddneville; pp. 25, 26, 29 : Carlos A. Merighe; pp. 32, 42: Rob Verhoeven; p. 34 top: meckhert; p. 39: auntjojo; pp. 43, 77, 207: Bomba Rosa; pp. 44, 46: antwerpenR; p. 45: David Ooms; p. 50: John Pavelka; p. 51: David Ooms; p. 66: Javier Aroche; p. 80: AmaretoCR: p. 84: Eric Menjivar; p. 113: rhurtubia; p. 119: Poldavo (Alex); p. 121: 00ucci; p. 122: clurr; p. 123: Bruno Girin; p. 133: meg and rahul; p. 139: David Ooms; p. 145: asorsz; p. 159 bottom: Cristobal Alvarado Minic; p. 165: anoldent; p. 166: qnr; p. 183: klaasmer; pp. 185, 188: Gusjer; p. 186: Walter Rodriguez; p. 201: AlphaTangoBravo/Adam Baker.

Note: the use of these photos does not represent an endorsement of this book or any services listed within by any of the photographers listed above.

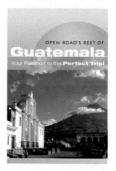